LETTING GOD PLAN YOUR FAMILY

LETTING GOD PLAN YOUR FAMILY

Samuel A. Owen, Jr.

CROSSWAY BOOKS•WHEATON, ILLINOIS
A DIVISION OF GOOD NEWS PUBLISHERS

Letting God Plan Your Family.

© Copyright 1990 by Samuel A. Owen, Jr.

Published by Crossway Books, a division of
Good News Publishers, Wheaton, Illinois 60187.

Cover photo: Ewing Galloway, Inc.

Cover design: Diane Fliehler

First printing, 1990

Printed in the United States of America

Library of Congress Catalog Card Number 90-80626

ISBN 0-89107-585-2

Unless otherwise noted, all Bible quotations are taken from *New American Standard Bible*, copyright © 1977 by the Lockman Foundation.

CONTENTS

PART 1

CONTRACEPTION: IS IT A PROBLEM?

CHAPTER 1

ASKING THE RIGHT QUESTION

He proposes, and she says yes. Suddenly their lives are filled with plans and decisions. Where will they be married, and by whom? Who will be in the bridal party, and what will they wear? What about flowers, cake, invitations, the honeymoon?

In addition to preparing for the ceremony, the starry-eyed couple begins planning for after the wedding. Where will they live? Will she continue to work full-time? How will they define their roles . . . Who will take out the garbage?

One evening, as they confirm details and dream together about their happily-ever-after, she realizes they've overlooked an important area. They have never seriously talked about having a family. So she broaches the subject. "You want children, don't you?"

"Sure. But not right away, of course."

"No, that would be too stressful. I've heard it's good to wait at least two years."

"That sounds wise," he agrees. "That will give us time to build a solid marriage."

"How many children do you want?"

"I guess two or three. I don't think I'll ever earn enough to feed a large family."

"I think two is a good number," she says. "The world is getting so overpopulated."

They sit quietly for a moment, and then he asks the next obvious question—the one considered by most couples: "What method of contraception will we use?"

After discussing the advantages and disadvantages of various means of contraception, and perhaps consulting pastors, family members, friends, or Christian marriage books, they agree on the method best suited for them.

The Neglected Question

While the dialogue may vary from couple to couple, the issue generally does not. Husbands and wives assume their right and responsibility to control the number and spacing of their children. It is a question of how, not if.

But what if a young man and woman take exception and do *not* assume their right to plan their family? What if, instead of discussing the method, Carl asks his fiancée, Sue, "Should we practice contraception?"

"Of course!" she quickly responds. "Otherwise I'm bound to get pregnant right away. You don't want that, do you?"

"But is it right to practice contraception?"

"Certainly! Everyone does it."

"Does that make it *right*?"

Sue hesitates for a moment. "No, I suppose not. I guess I've never really thought about it before."

"Me either, but we'd better think about it now. I'm going to ask my dad for his opinion."

The next day Carl stops by his parents' home and approaches the subject. "What do you think about contraception, Dad?"

"You mean, which method do I think is best?"

"No . . . Do you think we should practice contraception?"

"Definitely! The last thing you want is a baby nine months after your wedding night. Children are wonderful, but they're also a big responsibility."

"I realize that, but . . ."

"They're expensive too, especially for someone like you who just started a new job. Give yourselves a couple years to get your feet on the ground and your marriage off to a good start. Then think about a family."

"But . . ."

"Besides, I'm too young to be a grandfather." His father smiles.

Carl smiles back, though he does not feel satisfied. He doesn't want to know what is practical; he wants to know what is *right.* So he makes an appointment with their pastor.

Pastor Simpson extends a warm handshake to Carl and Sue as they enter his office. "The big day's just around the corner, isn't it. Bet you're sitting on pins and needles!"

"We're pretty excited," Sue agrees.

Carl grins and nods.

After motioning them to two chairs, Pastor Simpson

sits down behind his desk. "Well, what can I do for you today?"

Carl clears his throat. "This may sound silly, but I want to ask you about contraception."

"Yes, there are a lot of methods to choose from these days, aren't there."

"It's not the method I want to talk about. I'm wondering if we should even practice contraception."

"Well, I certainly recommend it. Marriage is a big enough adjustment in itself without adding parenthood. And you're just getting started in your career, aren't you, Carl?"

"Yes."

"How do you feel about this, Sue? Do you want to be a mother right away?"

"No . . . I imagine it will take me some time to get used to being a wife. Besides, I've got a good job too, and if I can keep working for a couple of years, we can buy a house."

"It sounds like it would be wise for you to wait to begin your family. Then try to give yourselves enough space in between so you aren't overwhelmed. Of course, accidents do happen—our first daughter came earlier than we had planned, and our son followed rather quickly. Naturally, we were thrilled to have them, and God gave us the grace. But you have the advantage of better methods, so you can plan more carefully."

Sue, pleased with the pastor's advice, changes the subject to wedding arrangements. Carl, however, still feels puzzled. He cannot deny that in light of their circumstances, practicing contraception seems logical. Yet he wonders, should they base their decision on their situation, or has God given another standard?

Pastor Simpson interrupts his thoughts. "You two are going to the marriage conference this weekend, aren't you? If you have any other questions, I expect the speakers will address them, and much more adequately than I could. Those two men are tops in the marriage field. But if you need to talk again later, please give me a call. I'd be glad to get together."

Carl and Sue stand up and thank him for his time. As they walk out into the sunshine, Carl hopes their pastor is right. He hopes his question will be answered that weekend.

When they arrive at the conference, Carl quickly scans the syllabus. Good—contraception is included in the seminar on sex. But when that hour arrives, he is disappointed. The description of the different methods is informative, but the speaker never answers Carl's question. The speaker recommends some books, however. So during the afternoon break, Carl checks the book table. He again feels let down. Several cover methods, but none mention the morality of contraception.

After they get into the car to leave, Carl turns to Sue. "I guess that settles it—practicing contraception must be O.K. After all, the experts never question it, so why should we? No one has said it is wrong, so it must be right."

Contraception: A Given

Once again contraception wins by default. Even Christians who question its morality interpret the evangelical church's silence as a nod of approval. This message is reinforced by those leaders who speak up and encourage family planning. Thus, because the "experts" endorse it, couples assume God's Word teaches that practicing contraception is valid.

Yet, as Christians should we assume anything? Should we blindly follow those who silently or verbally consent to contraception? No, we must test all things by Scripture and thereby develop convictions. We must take responsibility, knowing each of us is accountable to God in this and all issues of life. When we stand before Him, we cannot point to anyone else—no matter what their credentials—and say, "But he told me . . ." or "She said . . ." God will simply ask us if we knew and acted according to what *He* said.

Therefore, we must examine what God says. It is time to step off the well-traveled road and take a fresh, Biblical look at the moral dimension of contraception. We must seek God's perspective by asking, as this book does, "What saith the Scriptures?" If Christ should be Lord of all life, shouldn't He also be Lord of the womb?

But first we should understand more about the prevalent contraceptive attitude and how it evolved.

CHAPTER 2

THE DEVELOPMENT OF A CONTRACEPTIVE ATTITUDE

As eight-year-old Amanda and Nicole walk to school, they see a mother pushing her baby in a stroller. Amanda watches the baby for a moment, then turns to her friend and asks, "How many babies will you have when you get married?"

"I think I'll have three," Nicole answers. "How about you?"

"I'm going to have just two. My parents decided to have three," Amanda explains, shaking her head, "and they got my pesty little brother."

Family planning is a way of life for even the youngest members of our society. Long before they understand reproduction and contraception, they assume they will control if and when they have children. Their parents probably limited the number and planned the timing of their offspring, and they intend to do the same. After all, that seems to be how it is done in the world in which they live.

Yet, it has not always been that way. The contraceptive attitude so prevalent today was rare in the past. Until recently the world was for the most part pro-fertility. Children were considered blessings, barrenness a curse. In Genesis 16 we read that Sarai's desperate longing for children led her to give her maid, Hagar, to Abram in hopes she would bear children for Sarai. Another Israelite, Hannah, also longed for a child. "And she, greatly distressed, prayed to the LORD and wept bitterly" (1 Samuel 1:10).

In ancient Persia childlessness was said to be a curse, and the blessing of children was greatly desired. "In conformity with this desire, prayers and sacrifices were offered in the hopes of obtaining children."[1] The Chinese philosopher Confucius said, "There are three things which are unfilial, but the most unfilial of these is to have no sons."[2] The Chinese took heed and produced large families. And even into the twentieth century, Celts gladly welcomed the birth of children—boys and girls—and large families were common.[3] Other peoples held similar attitudes through the ages.

This is not to say birth control is totally new. Coitus interruptus has been used since ancient times, and Egyptian papyri dating between 1900 and 1100 B.C. give recipes for contraceptive preparations. For example, women were to sprinkle honey and sodium carbonate in the vulva, or put crocodile dung in the opening of the uterus.[4] Various other methods have been used in other societies. Until recent years, however, the practice of contraception was the great exception, and a desire for children prevailed.

The Birth of the Birth Control Movement

In the eighteenth century, the modern birth control movement began. It started in France with a strong but unorganized tendency to limit family size.[5] These efforts were aided by the vulcanization of rubber in 1843, which made rubber condoms available and inexpensive. Occlusive sponges also were available and recommended.[6]

While these devices certainly were more appealing than crocodile dung, they were not responsible for the increasing practice of contraception. Rather, the rise was prompted by the development of a humanistic attitude—an attitude that rejects the supernatural and focuses on human interests and capabilities. The greater accessibility of contraceptives was a result, not a cause, of that attitude.

Historian Jeremy Jackson has traced the genesis and evolution of this man-centered attitude over a 400-year period, from the Renaissance through the Enlightenment and into the present age.[7] He characterizes it as a "control mentality," a way of thinking resulting from a lost belief in God. "If man is the highest form of being, the responsibility for life falls upon man's shoulder."[8] Thus, people feel responsible to control life.

Man has expressed this desire and need to control by striving to improve and protect his standard of living. He advanced technologically and agriculturally to provide more food and other goods. He also found ways to limit the number of mouths to feed, bodies to clothe, and minds to educate. His control mentality led him to keep his standard of living high by keeping his family size low.

With this attitude prevailing, the birth control movement in France and England became organized in the nineteenth century. Its progenitors included Marquis de Condorcet, the influential champion of the perfectibility of humanity; anarchist William Godwin who, like Condorcet, believed in extremes of social progress; utilitarian Jeremy Bentham; and philosopher James Mill.[9]

The control mentality also resulted in organized promotion of contraception in the United States. In 1913 Margaret Sanger began the movement that led to the founding of the American Birth Control League, later known as the Planned Parenthood Federation of America. By 1933 most medical schools included instruction about contraception techniques. And throughout American society advocates for conception control won increasing support, basing their humanistic arguments on social good and personal happiness.[10]

Thus, the birth control movement was on the move. It became more widely accepted in Europe and the United States, and it soon spread to other countries. Throughout the world the practice of contraception continued to increase, motivated by a humanistic, man-is-in-control philosophy.

"Women Have Rights Too"

Certainly the control mentality has been a major force behind the rising practice of contraception, but it is not the only force. We must not overlook the effect of the women's movement.

This movement began after World War I, when

social restrictions in the Anglo-Saxon and Scandinavian world were lowered. Women, who had been unfairly restricted in various ways, began to rally for rights. Among their cries was the demand for birth control, shouted most loudly by Marie Stopes in England and Margaret Sanger in the United States.

The outcries continue. In the name of "rights" and "freedom," feminists expound the philosophy that a career is more fulfilling than motherhood, and that a woman can realize her full potential only by leaving home and getting a job. They have denied or ignored the Biblical pattern for women's roles, holding up instead the goal of emancipation from the family. It is claimed, "If women can be relieved of the bondage of childbirth, they can accede to their full humanity. And we all can escape the crucible of the family."[11]

Since motherhood is seen as bondage chains, contraception is hailed the release key. Thus, women are urged to prevent pregnancies, and when their efforts fail, to prevent their baby's birth. That is their right, or so the feminists assert. An increasing number of women have embraced this philosophy.

"I Owe It to Myself"

In addition to the control mentality and women's movement, another powerful factor contributing to the practice of contraception is the rise of narcissism. This philosophy, or religion, was named after the mythological youth Narcissus, who fell in love with his own reflection. Thomas Howard aptly calls it the cult of self.

A narcissist, among other things, "demands immediate gratification and lives in a state of restless, perpetually unsatisfied desire."[12] Can anyone deny that state of being prevails in our society today? It is estimated that nearly 80 percent of the population is frantically searching for self-fulfillment. "In place of the self-denial ethic that once ruled American life, we now find people who refuse to deny themselves *anything*—not out of bottomless appetite, but on the strange moral principle that 'I have a duty to myself.'"[13]

Inherent in this duty to self is a duty to control conception. After all, to bear and raise children, parents must deny themselves at least *some* things. They suddenly must consider someone else's needs, rather than focusing solely on their own desires. The price seems too high, so the narcissists avoid paying it by practicing contraception.

The Modern View of Children

The striving for self-fulfillment, the demand for rights, and the desire to control clearly have affected people's attitude toward the family. Marriage partners are increasingly self-centered and obsessed with sexual technique and pleasure. Even more significant, many have a definite, though sometimes subtle, anti-child attitude.

Feminist author and lecturer Germaine Greer writes, "Historically, human societies have been pro-child; modern society is unique in that it is profoundly hostile to children. We in the West do not refrain from childbirth because we are concerned about the population explosion or because we feel we cannot afford children, but because we do not like children."[14] She has stated in the extreme the sentiments commonly expressed in everyday life.

This mentality of not wanting children—at least not more than one or maybe two, and those only after the new car is paid for and some progress is made on the mortgage—is tied to the mentality of controlling life for one's convenience and pleasure. Husbands and wives seek personal fulfillment and various goals, and they resent any interference from children. They want to do what they want to do, and children can get in the way.

Children make work and can cause grief. Who wants to change diapers at 2 A.M. or try to discipline a rebellious teenager? Children also can be ruinously expensive, at least from the point of view of couples who prefer to spend their money on themselves. So children are prevented or limited. Those born, intentionally or "accidentally," often are resented as intruders. They are barriers to personal goals. This attitude is evident even in *Encyclopedia Britannica:* "Men have ambitions for social and economic position, higher living standards. . . . Such individual fulfillment probably has a better chance of success if income is concentrated on fewer children."[15]

Social and material concerns have taken precedent over home and family. Maternity, if allowed in the marriage at all, is assigned a low priority. It must take a backseat to "more important" matters.

This change in priorities has affected not only individual families, but our society as a whole. A Harvard Medical School professor notes, "The shift from spiritual to material values in our culture . . . has resulted in profound moral confusion."[16] This clearly is seen in the areas of marital roles, family relationships, and conception control.

Has the Church Been Affected?

Certainly nonbelievers have been influenced by the control mentality, the women's movement, and narcissism, but what about Christians? Hasn't the church kept its doors closed to this philosophical climate? Unfortunately not. The "me-first" mentality is corrupting not only the life of the nation but, to a shocking degree, the very soul of the evangelical church.[17]

This influence is evident in the area of conception control. The attitudes and actions of most Christians express their adherence to the quality-of-life ethic. Following the world average, they limit their families to 2.2 children. They also express a negative attitude toward large families.

> The expression of this attitude is unconsciously subtle: one is said to have "x" number of children because one doesn't believe in birth control. That is exactly the same as saying that I wear clothes because I don't believe in nudity. . . . Both of these parallel statements are true . . . But notice that these are negative definitions. There are positive reasons for wearing

> clothes and positive reasons for hav-
> ing large families. This, then, is what I
> mean by a negative or ambivalent atti-
> tude towards large families: not actual
> hostility, though this may sometimes
> be experienced, but defining a positive
> phenomenon in negative terms.[18]

This change in Protestant thinking regarding conception control is a recent development. Until early in
the twentieth century, "the ethos of Wittenberg and
Geneva and Canterbury was as strongly pro-fertility as
that of Rome."[19] Protestant, Catholic, and Orthodox leaders universally taught that interfering with the conception of life was a grave sin against God, not merely against
the church.[20]

The official teachings of the Anglican and Protestant
churches did not begin to change until the Lambeth
Conference of 1930. In 1908 and 1920 the conference
had disallowed the use of contraceptives, but in 1930 it
conceded that contraception might be morally legitimate in extremely limited circumstances. This was the
conference's first resolution to pass without a unanimous vote, and those who supported it most likely were
influenced by Margaret Sanger's Planned Parenthood
campaign. The world's influence continued, and in 1958
the Lambeth Conference unanimously approved the use
of contraceptives.[21]

It is remarkable to realize that *all Christian denominations*, whether Protestant or Catholic, *were com-*

pletely opposed to contraception as recently as sixty years ago.[22] And if this was the unanimous position of Christians throughout all the church's history except for the most recent decades, certainly it is worth considering if the church's reversal on contraception is in accord with God's will.

As with the world's attitude, the changing Protestant view was not based on the greater availability of contraceptives, but on a "rights" mentality of control.[23] This attitude is increasingly evident among Christians, as indicated by the following representative comments (emphasis added):

> For the sake of their marriage and the education of their children, the couples will not simply leave the creation of new life to *chance*.[24]

> ... we have a *right* to control conception.[25]

> Children today are an increasing economic *burden* and an increasing *personal burden* ... they put a drain upon the family *standard of living* rather than contributing to it. Men and women are *less willing* to have large families which limit their *freedom and opportunity to enjoy what modern life holds out to them*.[26]

As Christians, we cannot assume this new acceptance of contraception is wrong simply because it opposes the the view held by the church for hundreds of years. *But neither can we assume the new attitude is right.* Our perspective must be tested against Scripture. We must individually, in the power of the Holy Spirit, examine God's Word before adopting a viewpoint.

That does not mean the church's teaching has no value. God has revealed His truth to others besides ourselves, making our private judgment triangular: It involves God's mind, our mind, and the church's mind. Therefore, we should not only judge our personal conclusions by the Bible; we should compare them with the accumulated wisdom of the church.

But the bulk of our study must be in the Scripture, which we now will examine. We will see what God says about who should control the womb. Then, equipped with a knowledge of His perspective and the church's past and present attitude, we will be ready to draw our own conclusions regarding the practice of contraception.

PART 2

WHAT DOES THE BIBLE SAY?

CHAPTER 3

Marriage, Sex, and the Pursuit of Happiness

Few things in life are more frustrating than opening the box containing your newfangled whatchamagadget and finding no instructions. After turning the box over and over and inside out, you realize you are on your own. The manufacturer has left it up to you to determine how to assemble and operate his wonder creation. Several trials later, you conclude this is because the manufacturer himself has not figured out how it works.

Fortunately the Creator of mankind knows how we can and should function, and He has given us adequate directions. In His manual, the Bible, He tells us how to live and how to relate to Him and to the rest of His creation. He also makes it clear we must follow His instructions not only for our benefit, but for His glory. He is to be Lord of our lives—of every area. Thus, we must obey His Word, walking by faith in our wise, loving, sovereign God.

Of course, to obey His instructions regarding contraception, or any issue, we must learn what He says. How do we begin? Do we look up "contraception" in a concordance? No. The Bible does not include the word, just as the teachings applicable to pornography or abortion do not contain those words. We must dig a little deeper. We must study passages and principles that relate to contraception.

That is what we will do in this section. We will begin in this chapter with God's purposes for marriage and for sex. In Chapter 4 we will study His teaching on the place of children and the role of women. Then in Chapter 5 we will look at His overall perspective of life and how it relates to our convictions in this area. Our examination of these truths will lead us to the Biblical ideal regarding the practice of contraception.

The Purpose of Marriage

Marriage is good! Indeed, it is ordained by God and is to be gratefully enjoyed. We are not to reject the gift of this union, but are rather to receive it with thanksgiving (1 Timothy 4:3-5). While a few are called to celibacy, the whole tenor of Scripture is that wedlock is the usual course of life for the majority of men and women. It is, as Calvin said, "the bond which God has preferred to all others."[1] Amen!

But what is the purpose of this bond? Again, we can make no assumptions. We must come to grips with the teaching of Scripture regarding the purposes of marriage. Our conclusions will go a long way in helping us develop a perspective on conception control.

In Ephesians 5:22-33, Paul explains that marriage is an analogy of the relationship between Christ and His church. Like one who is weaving a fine tapestry, the apostle weaves together concepts regarding Christ and the church and regarding husband and wife. His teachings about Christ and His bride form the background for his teaching about marriage.

While this passage does not delineate the purposes of marriage, it highlights the central issue: marriage is ultimately for God. He intends for this relationship between a man and a woman to reveal truths about His relationship with His people. God's established roles for a husband and wife reveal that Christ is to be the Head, and we, the church, are to honor Him and submit to Him. The marriage union illustrates that we are one with Christ. Because we are members of His Body, He nourishes and cherishes us. Also, a godly husband's love for his wife exemplifies God's sacrificial love for the church, which Christ demonstrated on the cross. What is the motive for that love? According to this passage, Christ died so He could sanctify the church and present her holy and blameless to Himself. Clearly, the purpose of such love, and all of marriage, is God-centered, not self-centered.

The first two chapters of Genesis also present marriage as God-centered. God told man, "Be fruitful and multiply, and fill the earth, and subdue it" (1:28). Then, so Adam could accomplish this, He gave Eve to him as a helper (2:18-24). He instituted marriage for the outworking of His plan. God knew that apart from this matrimonial partnership, man could not fill the earth and rule over the rest of creation. Thus, He established marriage to advance *His* lordship, to fulfill *His* purposes.

From God's initial instructions in Genesis 1:28, we can see that God intends for husbands and wives to reproduce. They are to fill the earth with others who can glorify Him. Indeed, according to Genesis, a primary purpose for marriage is procreation.[2]

Other passages likewise teach that God has given married couples the responsibility of bearing children. In Genesis 9:1 God blesses Noah and his sons and says, "Be fruitful and multiply, and fill the earth," a command He repeats in verse 7. In 1 Timothy 5:14 Paul writes, "I want younger widows to get married, bear children . . ." Thus, while society calls children an unnecessary option, God's Word says bearing and raising children is an integral part of the marriage relationship.

This does not mean, however, that couples unable to have children have an imperfect marriage, are less fulfilled, or cannot be as effective in their lives and ministries. God blesses and uses infertile husbands and wives, but we must remember that their condition is His choice, not theirs. Childlessness has rightly been viewed as a burden allowed by the Lord in His inscrutable wisdom (cf. Luke 1:25). Couples who must bear that burden should seek God's wisdom for how to respond. He may lead them to compensate for their closed womb by opening their home and lives to neglected, forgotten, unwanted children, for example.

While procreation is a primary purpose of marriage, it is not the only one. According to Genesis 2:23-25, the other important purpose is the union of husband and wife. This one-flesh union encompasses the totality of each individual; it is physical, emotional, mental, spiritual. And, as we saw in Ephesians 5, this union is designed to reflect to the world a picture of God and His relationship with His people.

Thus, Scripture delineates procreation and unity as the two purposes of marriage. But what about pleasure and intimacy? Doesn't the Bible speak of these benefits of marriage? Shouldn't we include them on our list?

Scripture definitely speaks of pleasure and intimacy, but it presents them as blossoms on the flower of marriage, not as part of its root. Solomon writes, "Enjoy life with the woman whom you love all the days of your fleeting life which He has given to you under the sun; for this is your reward in life, and in your toil in which you have labored under the sun" (Ecclesiastes 9:9). In Proverbs 5:18, 19 he writes, "[R]ejoice in the wife of your youth. . . . Let her breasts satisfy you at all times; be exhilarated always with her love." These verses, as well as the Song of Solomon, indicate that pleasure and intimacy are benefits, rather than purposes, of marriage.

Some also have suggested that God established marriage as a cure for loneliness. If you are a husband or wife who knows the joy of your spouse's companionship, you might readily agree. The text of Genesis 1 and 2, however, indicates Adam's problem was not loneliness but incompleteness. Just as the creation of the animals was finished only after God had made them all, the creation of man was complete only after He had created male and female. Making Adam was not enough; he needed Eve.

In fact, Adam needed more than Eve—he needed a

household, a society, a people. Thus, God did not simply provide a wife; He provided a wife with whom Adam could beget children and establish a family.[3] This, of course, brings us back to one of the two primary purposes of marriage: procreation.

As we consider pleasure, intimacy, companionship, and any other suggested purpose for marriage, we must remember that this God-instituted relationship is to be God-centered. We need to beware of the me-centered mentality outlined in Chapter 2 and cling to the Biblical perspective. Rather than asking, "What can I gain from this union?" we should ask, "How can and should God benefit?"

That does not negate these fringe benefits of marriage; instead, it puts them in their proper place. They are like a gift from our employer in appreciation for a job well done. Our purpose for performing the task was not to receive the gift, but we will gratefully enjoy it. Similarly, we must not view the benefits of marriage as goals. If we do, we never will achieve them. Rather, we must see these benefits as by-products of following God's design and of seeking to glorify Him. Then, and only then, will we experience the maximum pleasure, intimacy, and companionship possible in our marriage, because we are living according to His perfect plan.

> Christian marriage . . . is God-centered
> (producing what God wants) rather
> than me- or us-centered (meeting my
> or our desires). As with all of God's

designs, our needs do get met, but by the route of faith. First we do what God commands; then to our surprise we find ourselves blessed. We deny ourselves and take up our cross, and then we find the burden light and pleasant. Then we find ourselves. Then we find our hearts set free, and the love of God shed abroad in our hearts, and our marriages blossoming and blooming.[4]

The Purpose of Sex

These conclusions about marriage also apply to sex. Just as God's gift of marriage is good, so is His gift of sex. Our Creator designed it to be part of a healthy marriage. In Genesis 2:24 we read, "For this cause a man shall leave his father and his mother, and shall cleave to his wife; and they shall become one flesh." While this one-flesh union is not limited to the physical, it certainly includes it. Sexual intercourse is a vital part of marriage, and, as Paul taught in 1 Corinthians 7:1-5, it should be enjoyed regularly.

Undeniably, sex meets very important needs for the husband and wife and their relationship. It fulfills their desires and hinders them from immorality (1 Corinthians 7:2-5). Sex relieves the tensions of life and at the same time releases creative energies in both partners. The physical union also expresses the couple's bond of committed love. And sex brings mutual enjoyment and pleasure (Proverbs 5:18, 19; Song of Solomon).

But these elements of the sexual relationship are benefits rather than purposes. As with marriage, the purposes of sex are the one-flesh unity and the procreation of children, who beautifully illustrate the "one-flesh" union. God made clear this priority of reproduction when He commanded us to "Be fruitful and multiply, and fill the earth" (Genesis 1:28).

Even our anatomy indicates that procreation is a primary purpose of sex. The man is designed to contribute his sperm; the woman is designed to receive it for impregnation. Her uterus is intended for carrying and nurturing the new life during gestation, her breasts for nurturing the child after birth. God made our sexual organs capable of erotic stimulation, but that is meant to lead to procreation. Such pleasure is not to be an end in itself.[5]

Thus, God's Word and His creation teach that His goal for our sexuality is to beget children, the fruit of marital love, and thus populate the earth. This primary purpose must not be softened or ignored. Certainly we can—and should—enjoy pleasure and the other benefits of the sexual act, but we must see them only as benefits. We must not enthrone pleasure as the ultimate goal and separate reproduction from the sexual act. If we do distort God's purposes in this way, we will suffer the consequences. As P. E. Hughes explains, this would be "the perversion of sex to selfish and licentious ends which will soon pall in surfeit and disgust."[6]

Strong words? Yes, but their strength is needed in this day when many view sex, and all of life, as man-centered rather than God-centered. We need to turn our focus to God and to His Biblically-defined purposes for sex and marriage.

Answering the Critics

Despite Scripture's teachings that procreation is a primary purpose of marriage and sex, some Christians have relegated it to a secondary and seemingly insignificant position. They have then concluded that limiting conception is legitimate.

> ... procreation is not the primary purpose of marriage. Consequently, the marital act is even less bound to the purpose of procreation. The decision in regard to procreation is a free ethical decision, insofar as the husband and wife are concerned.[7]

> ... if sex is not merely for propagation, then there is no reason why one cannot enjoy the other purposes of sex without producing children.[8]

> If then, sexual intercourse has non-procreative ends, marital partners have the right to control conception.[9]

Such statements abound in Christian literature, but that does not make them true. Rather, they seem to be an overreaction to the position that marriage was *only* for procreation, as taught by some early Church Fathers and often stressed in the Roman Catholic Church. This earlier view also was an overreaction; the church was countering the Gnostic, Stoic, and similar heresies regarding marriage and sex. But we cannot throw out the Church Fathers' conclusion about contraception simply because they had an inadequate view of marriage. Again, we must consider the Biblical data.

We also should ask, Do these modern statements make sense? Do these writers' conclusions follow the premise logically? No, they do not. Just because procreation is not the only purpose of marriage and sex, that does not mean it is not *a* purpose, deserving equal consideration. Nor does it automatically legitimize limiting conception. If we followed this pattern of "logic," we could say eating has three purposes: survival, good health, and pleasure. Since survival is not the only reason for eating, we need not seek to survive by eating. In fact, we can eat only for pleasure—we can limit our diet to chocolate bars if we wish.

The crux of the matter is, the purposes of the marriage relationship cannot be separated. Marriage and sex are not just for procreation; neither are they just for unity. They are for both. Bruce Waltke notes, "Protestant theologians often justify birth control by separating these purposes of marriage from one another. But according to the Old Testament, the Creator instituted marriage to serve all these ends together."[10]

We must be careful not to follow the example of

those who separate these purposes. Such a distortion may fit what we want to believe, but it does not fit with what God says. If we follow instead the Biblical teaching on the purposes of marriage and sex, then we can see that relationship as God intended it. We also will begin to gain God's perspective on contraception.

Did God Really Command Us?

In addition to separating the purposes of the marriage union, some Christians have limited the scope of God's command to "Be fruitful and multiply, and fill the earth" (Genesis 1:28). They assert that God has commanded the human race to multiply, but He does not require *every* member of it to reproduce. Therefore, they conclude, contraception is permissible.

Again, we must examine the Scriptural basis and the logic of this argument. Yes, it is true that not every individual is commanded to reproduce. We know from 1 Corinthians 7 that marriage is not mandated, and we know God commands the unmarried to abstain from sexual intercourse. Thus, we can conclude that celibates are not to reproduce. But how can we jump to the conclusion that not all married couples are called to bear children? As we have seen, Scripture teaches that procreation is a primary purpose of their union.

"But Genesis 1:28 does not say how many offspring couples are to bear or when they are to start their family," some argue. Therefore, they assume, man is to determine this.[11] Again, such a conclusion is unwarranted. Just because God did not give us specifics regarding the number and timing of children does not mean He put us in control of their conception. Has He put us in charge of the number and timing of our "spiritual children?" That is, can we claim to control when and how many people come to new life in Christ through our influence? Neither can we argue from Scripture's silence that we are in control of the number and timing of our physical children. Rather, we must consider the relevant Biblical data.

Others have suggested that the command has been fulfilled—the earth is full. But who says? In fact as we shall see in later chapters, the whole idea of "overpopulation" is a serious distortion. No passage of Scripture indicates that the job is done or that God has rescinded His command. (Does man ever have the authority to decide this?) The burden of proof lies with those who wish to prove that the earth is full and that the mandate is no longer valid.

But is Genesis 1:28 truly a command? Some prefer to call it a blessing, thus giving man the choice of whether or not to bear children.[12] Again, we run into a partial truth. Yes, the verse begins, "And God blessed them," but Scripture does not divorce blessing from command. Rather, it ties the two together. Blessing and responsibility go hand in hand. "To bless is to bestow not only a gift but a function."[13]

This union of blessings and functions is clear in many passages. After God created the fish and the birds, He "blessed them, saying, 'Be fruitful and multiply'" (Genesis 1:22). He blessed the seventh day and made it holy, and He gave a specific command for keeping it holy (Genesis 2:3;

Exodus 20:8-11). When God established His covenant with Abraham, He commanded him and his descendants to be circumcised, and He said He would bless Sarah and give them a son through her (Genesis 17). In other words, He would bless her by making her fertile so she could fulfill her God-appointed function—so they could produce a nation set apart for His glory. When God blessed Jacob, He commanded him, "Be fruitful and multiply" (Genesis 35:9-12).

In these Scriptures, we cannot separate the blessing from the command or function. Nor can we view Genesis 1:28 as exclusively a blessing or exclusively a command. We must recognize it as both.

Seeing the bearing of children as a blessing *and* a command brings the focus back on God. While man obviously is involved in the process, the blessing ultimately rests with God and reflects His goodness.

> While not contesting the causal relationship between sexual intercourse and conception the Bible denies that the effect is inevitable or that parents have the power to bring about conception. The Bible preserves a deep respect for the mystery of fertilization, and urges a sense of thankfulness to God by emphasizing that the gift of a child is a divine blessing.[14]

Clearly, God is the giver of all life, blessing a couple with children as He sees fit. He is ultimately responsible for the number and timing of offspring. We, in return, should bless Him for His good gifts, not refusing them, resenting them, or taking them for granted. We should thank our gracious Lord for children—His divine blessings.

We will now turn our attention to those blessings. Having examined God's perspective on marriage and sex, we will take a look at the fruit of the marriage union. We will see what Scripture teaches about the place of children and also will study the role of women. Our conclusions in both these areas will help us progress toward a Biblical view of contraception.

CHAPTER 4

THE PLACE OF CHILDREN AND WOMEN

> Children are a burden; the fruit of the
> womb is a curse. Like thorny sticks or
> burning embers in your hands, so are
> children. How fortunate is the couple
> who avoids having any.

That is how our society would have written Psalm 127:3-5. After all, from the day of their birth those bundles of "innocence" turn relatively carefree men and women into slaves to another's needs. Children hinder their parents' careers, their economic advancement, their fun . . . even their sex life.[1] Thus, husbands and wives should avoid these "unnecessary and undesirable intrusions"—or so the world says.

But what does God say? What is the Biblical perspective on children and their place in the marriage relationship?

God Has Commanded

First, as we saw in Chapter 3, God commands married couples to have children. He told Adam and Eve, "Be fruitful and multiply, and fill the earth" (Genesis 1:28), and then He repeated the command to Noah (Genesis 9:1, 7). Since God has not revoked these commands, they still stand today.

Thus, while marriage is optional (1 Corinthians 7), those who choose to wed are not given the option of whether or not to bear children. Procreation is a primary purpose of their marriage and sexual relationship. Their union is designed for and fulfilled in the birth of children. If couples do remain childless, it must be God's choice, not theirs. (Of course, He may also lead them to adopt.)

Children Are a Gift

God also says:

> Behold, children are a gift of the LORD; the fruit of the womb is a reward. Like arrows in the hand of a warrior, so are the children of one's youth. How blessed is the man whose quiver is full of them. (Psalm 127:3-5)

Clearly, God's perspective opposes the world's philosophy. Rather than seeing children as a curse, He describes them as a blessing. "Your wife shall be like a fruitful vine, within your house, your children like olive plants around your table. Behold, for thus shall the man be blessed who fears the LORD" (Psalm 128:3, 4).

Jacob, who bore twelve sons, knew he was blessed. When he and Esau were reunited after many years, Esau asked who all his brother's companions were. Jacob answered, "The children whom God has graciously given your servant" (Genesis 33:5).

Of course, at times even Christian parents are tempted to think of their children as anything but blessings. When their toddler throws a temper tantrum in the grocery store or spills a full cup of grape juice on the neighbor's new carpet, Mom and Dad may wonder how a "blessing" can be so trying.

Yet, children are not the only gifts that can require work and produce frustration. Ask any woman who has received the sewing machine she longed for . . . and then spent hours stitching and ripping seams. Will she throw out her sewing machine? Never! Or ask a man who was given the jigsaw and drill of his dreams. Despite late nights at his workbench and his grumblings about too-short boards and too-large holes, he never will part with his treasured tools.

Gifts can present a challenge and require work. In the spiritual realm, consider the gift of salvation. Certainly it is free; yet it results in our taking up our cross and following Christ (Matthew 10:38). As recipients of the gift, we become servants of the Giver.

The Bible also teaches that as Christians we receive spiritual gifts such as teaching, exhortation, giving, mercy, and serving. Does that mean we must do nothing, or that we have no further responsibility? Of course not. Paul writes, "And since we have gifts that differ according to the grace given to us, let each exercise them accordingly" (Romans 12:6).

Likewise, God describes children as a gift, but also recognizes that they are a responsibility. "And it is not untypical of God's gifts that first they are liabilities, or at least responsibilities, before they become obvious assets. The greater their promise, the more likely that these sons will be a handful before they are a quiverful."[2]

God knows parents face a challenge, so He gives instruction for raising children. He teaches, "Foolishness is bound up in the heart of a child; the rod of discipline will remove it far from him" (Proverbs 22:15). His Word also admonishes, "And, fathers, do not provoke your children to anger; but bring them up in the discipline and instruction of the Lord" (Ephesians 6:4).

The fact that children require work and are a responsibility, however, does not diminish their value as a precious gift. They truly are a "reward" (Psalm 127:3) and blessing from God. This leads us to a third point regarding a Biblical perspective of children.

God Opens and Closes the Womb

Many will readily agree that God is sovereign . . . until they enter a discussion on the practice of contraception. Yet Scripture clearly teaches that God's providence includes the womb. He is said to open it (Genesis 29:31; 30:22) and to close it (Genesis 20:18; 1 Samuel 1:5). In Old Testament times, people recognized this and acknowledged it was God's place to give or not give children.

> Now when Rachel saw that she bore
> Jacob no children, she became jealous

of her sister; and she said to Jacob,
"Give me children, or else I die." Then
Jacob's anger burned against Rachel,
and he said, "Am I in the place of God,
who has withheld from you the fruit of
the womb?" (Genesis 30:1, 2)

Throughout the Bible, this mentality is evident among God's people. Children were seen as gifts of a God who is in control—not the mere product of virility and fertility. They clearly saw each birth as the result of His handiwork. God is seen among His people, for example, as giving children when and as He chooses (Genesis 18:9-15); as compensation (29:31-34); and to take away reproach (30:22, 23). And He is the One who prevents conception from taking place (16:2). Note the following clear references as other samples of this truth:[3]

God waited until Abraham was a hundred years old and Sarah was ninety, long past the age of childbearing (Genesis 17:15-17; 18:11).

He gave Isaac and Rebekah twins in response to Isaac's prayer (Genesis 25:21, 24).

He also answered Hannah's prayer by opening her womb (1 Samuel 1:10, 20).

In the New Testament account of Zacharias and Elizabeth, we also see that God providentially controls the womb: "And they were both righteous in the sight of God, walking blamelessly in all the commandments and requirements of the Lord. And they had no child, because Elizabeth was barren, and they were both advanced in years. . . . But the angel said to him, '. . . your petition has been heard, and your wife Elizabeth will bear you a son, and you will give him the name John'" (Luke 1:6, 7, 13).

In addition to controlling if or when couples conceive children, God also determines when their "quiver is full" (Psalm 127:5). Some Christians have argued that because a quiver held four arrows, a full family has four children. We need not look far in Scripture, however, to see that God gives different families different numbers of children. Abraham and Sarah had one son, Isaac; Jacob had twelve sons; Job had seven sons and three daughters (and after they were killed, he had another seven sons and three daughters). In passages such as these that refer to specific numbers of children and in Psalm 127:5, "completeness—a completeness determined by God—is central."[4]

Thus, Scripture teaches that the absence or presence of children in a marriage, and the number of children present, is under God's providential control.

> What is perhaps most important in the biblical data regarding procreation is the clear sovereignty of God in childbirth. Man may talk about "accidents" and "birth control," but it is clear . . . that God is in control of fertility. In all of this, it is quite obvious in the Scriptures that parents are to consider themselves stewards of children who belong ultimately to God (Exodus

22:29; 34:19). Children are "from the Lord" and belong to Him.[5]

People talk of planning their family, but the Bible teaches that God is ultimately responsible for such planning. "Unless the LORD builds the house, they labor in vain who build it" (Psalm 127:1). In Hebrew, "to build a house" means "to construct a dwelling" and "to raise a family."[6] And, as the psalmist then explains, when God does build a family—when He gives a husband and wife children—they experience blessing, security, and honor.

In light of the Biblical teaching that God commands husbands and wives to have children, that those children are a blessing—a gift, and that God is providentially in control of the womb,[7] we must ask ourselves these questions:

1) Can we not trust a sovereign, good, wise God to give us the right number of children (if any) at the right time?

2) Who are we to refuse a gift or to tell the giver when we want it?

3) Whose job is it to determine the size of the "quiver" (Psalm 127:5)?

4) If children are a blessing, why don't we want to have them? "If the Bible says children are a blessing (and it does) but we don't see it that way, the fault lies in us."[8]

5) Finally, have we in this area jumped from a God-centered mentality to a self-centered mentality?

Rather than see children through the world's eyes, we must choose to accept God's perspective. We must respond to these questions in light of the Scriptural teaching about the place of children in marriage. As we do, our answers will greatly affect how we view contraception.

The Wife's Role

To develop convictions about contraception, we also must consider the Biblical teaching concerning women. What is their role in marriage and the family? Our society advocates that men and women have no distinct roles. "The leaders of the so-called women's liberation movement insistently demand that women be 'liberated' from what has hitherto been regarded as their distinctively womanly role in society as homemakers and bearers and raisers of children. Indeed, the home is denounced as a prison from which woman must be set free."[9] But what does the Bible say?

Again, we see that these modern notions oppose God's teaching. From the beginning of time God gave men and women distinct roles. He created woman as a "helper suitable for him" (Genesis 2:18). She was the solution for man's aloneness and incompleteness. God created the woman to be a helper who corresponded to man, who complemented him in the outworking of God's purposes.

This does not mean woman are inferior, but rather that they have a different function. "'Complementarity' implies an equality, a correspondence between man and woman. It also implies a difference. Woman complements man in a way that makes her a helper to him. Her role is not identical to his."[10]

After the Fall, God's conversation with Adam and Eve again points to distinct roles. With the woman He addresses childbirth and her submissive relationship to her husband, with the man his toil in his vocation (Genesis 3:16-19).

Several New Testament passages further clarify the role of wives. Older women are to train young wives "to love their husbands, to love their children, to be sensible, pure, workers at home, kind, being subject to their own husbands, that the word of God may not be dishonored" (Titus 2:4, 5). Paul also instructs "younger widows to marry, to have children, to manage their homes" (1 Timothy 5:14, NIV).

Scripture does not forbid a wife to leave the house or to take a concern for anything outside the home, but the home clearly is to be the center of her concern. This in no way relegates her to a second-class status or bondage, as some would have us believe. Instead, it puts her in her God-given role as a wife. It enables her to fulfill God's design for the home and family.

A woman's role as homemaker gives her an important sphere of authority. She is in charge of all the domestic arrangements. She must provide for the care and well-being of the whole family. A wife's responsibilities include planning and organizing her household and training and instructing her children. Anyone who has read Proverbs 31:10-31 knows that her role is anything but mundane. She is active and significant, and she faces continual challenges.

Inherent in this home-centered role is the bearing of

children. In addition to Genesis 1:28 and the Scriptures just mentioned, two other New Testament passages directly relate to the wife's role.

First, in 1 Timothy 2:15 Paul writes that "women shall be preserved through the bearing of children if they continue in faith and love and sanctity with self-restraint." Looking at the context, we see that he has just instructed men to pray and has told women they must not hold the office of teacher in the church.

Mary Pride writes:

> The next logical question would be, "Well then, what *can* women do for God if they are not supposed to teach?" Paul says that by persevering in our God-given role—childbearing—with a godly attitude, we will be saved. "Childbearing" sums up all our special biological and domestic functions. This is the exact same grammatical construction as Paul's advice to Timothy that Timothy should persevere in his life and doctrine, "because if you do, you will save both yourself and your hearers" (1 Tim. 4:16 [NIV]). Timothy's particular path to heavenly glory was his preaching and example. Ours is homeworking, all revolving around our role of childbearing.[11]

To use other Pauline terminology, the apostle is giving a particular in the "working out" of a woman's salvation (Philippians 2:12). Just as Timothy's working out of his salvation focused on his preaching, a woman works out her salvation by fulfilling her ordained role. She is to cultivate her highest call of homemaking and childbearing, which goes beyond giving birth and encompasses all her maternal duties. With willingness and a godly, thankful attitude, she is to fulfill her function, with all dignity.

The second passage that speaks of childbearing as a wife's calling, not just an optional extra, is 1 Timothy 5:14, 15 (NIV): "So I counsel younger widows to marry, to have children, to manage their homes and to give the enemy no opportunity for slander. Some have in fact already turned away to follow Satan."

In these verses we see a ramification of women not fulfilling their God-given role: the enemy can gain a foothold. Thus, Paul's advice to young widows is linked to his desire to safeguard the church's testimony. That desire also is evident in his admonition to women tempted to usurp authority in the assembly (1 Timothy 2:11-15) and in his general instruction to all women in Titus 2:3-5, which has the goal that "the word of God may not be dishonored."

Clearly, no woman should take God's instructions lightly. Before a wife rejects her Biblical role and accepts a more contemporary viewpoint, she should consider the consequences. She must recognize that her decision will affect not only herself and her family, but also God's Kingdom.

Has God Revised the Wife's Role?

Some argue that the Biblical teaching about the wife's role is cultural and therefore no longer binding on twentieth-century Christians. "Times have changed," they cry. True, but God's Word has not, and nothing in the context of these passages leads to a cultural interpretation. On the contrary, Paul bases his instruction on creation—not on the culture of his day.

The burden of proof lies with those who argue for a cultural interpretation, and it is doubtful their case will hold up in court. First, while the women in Paul's day generally were homemakers, they were much more "emancipated" than we might imagine. "The Roman matron, particularly during the late Republic and early empire, thus enjoyed greater freedom than any other woman in the ancient world . . . Conservatives longed for a return to the 'good old days,' when women knew their place."[12] Thus, if Paul's teaching had been cultural, we could expect it to be more liberal.

Second, it is illogical to isolate one portion of instruction as culturally irrelevant while accepting the remainder. If we say that "workers at home" (Titus 2:5) no longer applies, it follows that older women no longer need to be "reverent in their behavior . . . teaching what is good" (2:3). Likewise, we can assume they are free to be "malicious gossips" and "enslaved to much wine" (2:3). Of course, the instruction to young women to "love their husbands, to love their children, to be sensible, pure . . . kind" (2:4, 5) also must be cultural and therefore ignored. Do we really believe this is what God has in mind for wives?

In arguing against a home-centered role for wives, some Christians also point to Scriptural examples of women who worked outside the home. Again, the evidence does not substantiate the position. Yes, Lydia was a "seller of purple fabrics" (Acts 16:14), but did she run her business from outside or inside her home? Was she even married? In Acts 16:40 we see no mention of a husband, but rather it says "the house of Lydia." The Bible does not indicate she had a family. Similarly, Priscilla worked in tentmaking with her husband (Acts 18:3), but again it may have been a home-craft business. Also, we have no evidence God had given them children. In light of their traveling with Paul (Acts 18:18), it is doubtful they did have children to care for at that time.

But what about Proverbs 31? The woman described in this passage often is extolled as the counterpart to the modern career woman, but the text paints quite the opposite picture. She clearly is a woman who adorns herself "by means of good works, as befits women making a claim to godliness" (1 Timothy 2:10). She builds and manages her household and busily works at home, as instructed in Proverbs 14:1, 1 Timothy 5:14, and Titus 2:5. In other words, Proverbs 31 does not laud a career woman; it exalts a wife who carries out her domestic duties in the fear of the Lord and for the good of her family.

> The whole emphasis of the poem is on the benefits which the wife will bring to her husband and family by her industry and reliability. Behind it all lies the

sense of importance attached by the
ancient Israelite to the welfare and rep-
utation of the family: material prosper-
ity and good standing in the
community go together, and a good
wife is necessary to their achieve-
ment.[13]

That does not mean every woman must accomplish
all that is attributed to this "ideal" wife in Proverbs 31.
But all wives can follow her example. They need not pos-
sess her varied gifts and abilities in order to do their
domestic work for the good of their family, which according to Scripture is what God intends.

Still, the critics raise one final objection: "A home-
and family-centered role puts wives in bondage and
leaves them unfulfilled." After all, the world says, women
will find fulfillment in a "meaningful career." At least
some in the world say that—others say fulfillment comes
from material possessions, relationships, leisure, or
recreation.

Again we must ask, what does God say is the key to
fulfillment? As Christians, we must step off the shifting
sands of our society and plant our feet firmly on the Rock.

The Christian woman should not be
deceived by feminist dreams and
promises. Women will not automatically become immune to *anomie* [the
feeling one's life is meaningless] when

they are given equal opportunity in the work world. . . . The Christian who lacks fulfillment lacks it because he or she is sinning by not fixing his or her mind and trust on Christ, the only one who fulfills.[14]

Our quest for a meaningful life will be successful only as we seek and obey our Lord. Contrary to what the world says, His plan for us is fulfilling, not frustrating. The God who created us knows best how we should function. Therefore, we are wise to follow the Bible's teaching on the role of women, recognizing that role generally focuses on the home and on bearing and raising children. God may choose for an individual wife not to bear children, but Scripture indicates we must leave that choice to *Him*. We must trust God in this area, and in each area of our lives, if we wish to experience fulfillment.

Accepting the Biblical teaching on children and women also brings us one step closer to a Biblical perspective on contraception. Now we will take our final step. We will look at what God, through the Scriptures, says about life.

CHAPTER 5

GOD'S PERSPECTIVE ON LIFE

Two men shared a dark, damp prison cell. Their only contact with the outside world was a nine-inch-square window high on the cell wall. So each day they took turns standing on a chair and gazing out that window.

One man eagerly looked forward to his turn to look out into the open spaces. Every time he climbed down from the chair he was smiling and felt he could face a few more hours of confinement within the stone walls. The countenance of the other man, however, never changed. If anything, his heart seemed heavier after taking his turn at the window.

This puzzled the first man. Finally he asked his cellmate how he could remain so dreary after watching the birds fly across the sky. Didn't he enjoy seeing fluffy clouds move overhead through the blue expanse? Didn't he see in those clouds the shapes of animals, places, or other reminders of happier times? And how could he not feel brighter after drinking in the sunshine?

"What are you talking about? There are no birds or clouds or sky or sunshine outside that window," responded the second man. "There's only a gray asphalt yard, gray rats that run across it, and the gray walls and barbed wire that surround it. The world outside that window is just as dismal as the one in here."

These two men looked out the same window, but they saw two drastically different scenes. They had very opposing perspectives. Similarly, we have a choice of how we will see life. We can adopt the world's perspective or God's perspective. We can choose the distorted viewpoint communicated by our society or the truth as revealed in God's Word. As with these men, the perspective we choose will greatly affect our attitude.

So let's explore the second option: God's perspective. Specifically, we will consider four Scriptural truths about life.[1] These, in turn, will lead us to a Biblical conclusion about the practice of contraception.

Children: A Gift or a Threat?

As we learned in Chapter 4 *life is a gift from God.* Scripture shows that He providentially governs the womb, where life forms. He gives life or withholds it if and when He chooses. The giving of life is His prerogative and for His purposes and glory.

Those who desire children easily accept this perspective. One husband and wife I know, who prayed for years that God would open her womb, overflowed with gratitude toward God when He answered. They clearly saw the newly-forming life as a precious gift.

Those who focus on the diminished personal freedom and added responsibilities of raising children, however, may find it difficult to see the conception of life as
a gift. Like the man in the prison cell, the world outside
their window looks gray and dismal. But it need not
appear that way. If they will lift their eyes and see the
beauty and joy of God's creation and open their ears to
the reality of His Word, then they will understand that life
truly is a gift.

The second principle, which follows closely on the
first, is that *life is not a curse or a threat.* Granted, the pain
experienced in childbirth is a curse (Genesis 3:16), but
the fruit of childbirth is not. That new life, as we have
seen, is a gift.

He Never Promised Us a Rose Garden

Since children are a gift, not a curse, we can expect them
to bring us only fun, pleasure, a happily-ever-after existence . . . right? Wrong. While life definitely is a blessing,
our third Scriptural principle teaches that *life also is a
discipline.*

If you already have children, you may be nodding
your head and remembering the last time you applied
the board of education to your youngster's seat of learn-
ing. And certainly disciplining our sons and daughters is
an important part of our role as parents. But that is not
the discipline we will focus on now. Rather, we will consider how God uses children to discipline *us.*

Discipline (*paideuo, paideia*) is the process by

which we are taught. It is the way we learn, the way our characters are molded. The main purpose of discipline is to move us toward godly living.

As such, discipline is not limited to our offspring, but applies to all of God's children. "For those whom the Lord loves He disciplines; and He scourges every son whom He receives. . . . But if you are without discipline, of which all have become partakers, then you are illegitimate children and not sons" (Hebrews 12:6, 8).

If we are God's children, if we have been born again into His family through Jesus Christ, then we should readily accept our Father's discipline. "He disciplines us for our good, that we may share His holiness" (Hebrews 12:10).

In Proverbs, we also read of the value of receiving discipline:

> My son, do not reject the discipline of
> the LORD; or loathe His reproof, for
> whom the LORD loves He reproves,
> even as a father the son in whom he
> delights. (3:11, 12)

> Whoever loves discipline loves knowl-
> edge, but he who hates reproof is
> stupid. (12:1)

> A wise son accepts his father's disci-
> pline, but a scoffer does not listen to
> rebuke. (13:1)

He who neglects discipline despises
himself, but he who listens to reproof
acquires understanding. (15:32)

Listen to counsel and accept discipline, that you may be wise the rest of
your days. (19:20)

Cease listening, my son, to discipline,
and you will stray from the words of
knowledge. (19:27)

Do we want wisdom, knowledge, understanding?
Do we want to fully experience our Heavenly Father's
love? Then we must accept His discipline. It is essential to
the maturing process. Even Jesus, who was God Himself,
was "perfected" during His incarnation. "[A]lthough He
was a Son, He learned obedience from the things which
He suffered; and having been made perfect, He became
to all those who obey Him the source of eternal salvation"
(Hebrews 5:8, 9).

Despite the Biblical teaching on its necessity and
value, we tend to cringe at the thought of being disci-
plined. That is our human nature. We do not want to suffer, even though we know it will help us and, most
importantly, glorify God. Nor do we want to lower ourselves and admit our need to be changed. Yet, when we
consider what Christ endured for our sakes, and when we
remember that God is the potter and we are but the clay,
how can we possibly reject His discipline.

To benefit from discipline, we must put aside our own interests and focus on God's. We must humble ourselves and exalt our Father. "The fear of the LORD is the instruction for wisdom, and before honor comes humility" (Proverbs 15:33). With this attitude of fear and humility, we can willingly endure a process that is not always pleasant and experience a result that is very pleasant—closer conformity to the image of Christ.

The Potter's Tools

Just as a potter uses several tools in crafting a beautiful vase, God uses various tools to mold us. One of these tools is children. We learn responsibility as we care for our infant's every need. Our toddler's barrage of "why" questions teaches us patience. When our child colors the dining-room wallpaper, we learn self-control.

Through the gift of children, we also learn self-sacrifice. Most of us, no matter what our income, must make financial sacrifices. We also must sacrifice our freedom to go wherever we want whenever we want. In various ways we must deny ourselves and give ourselves to the new life entrusted to us.

As with all discipline, the discipline that occurs through our children may not sound appealing. We do not naturally want to give up any pleasure, self-gratification, or comfort . . . especially for the rigors of child-raising. "The long drawn-out discipline of family life is unusually demanding and humbling and formative. It is, perhaps, the most comprehensive of all disciplines and, therefore, the one we would most like to curtail."[2]

And it is an area of discipline we feel able to avoid—through the practice of contraception. Yet, we must remember again that God is the potter, we are the clay. Who are we to say how and when He can conform us? Who are we to try to limit the tools He uses to mold us to the image of Christ? Just as we should not reject the gift of life, we should not reject the discipline of life. We can and should trust our Heavenly Father, in His perfect wisdom and love, to discipline us only for our good and to use the tools *He* desires for accomplishing *His* purposes.

If We Can't Trust God . . .

The fourth Scriptural principle, which ties the others together, is that *life is to be lived by faith.* This means more than trusting Christ once and for all for our salvation; it means continually trusting God in every area of our lives.

Throughout the Bible this principle is evident. In Habakkuk 2:4 we read, "But the righteous will live by his faith." Jesus chastised Peter for his lack of faith (Matthew 14:31), and He commended the Canaanite woman, saying her faith was great (Matthew 15:28). In Hebrews 11, often called "The Hall of Faith," we read numerous examples of Old Testament men and women who demonstrated their trust in God. We also read, "And without faith it is impossible to please Him, for he who comes to God must believe that He is, and that He is the rewarder of those who seek him" (Hebrews 11:6).

Faith, which the writer of Hebrews defines as "the

assurance of things hoped for, the conviction of things not seen" (11:1), expresses reliance on the character of God. We live by faith because we know God is dependable. He always keeps His promises. We also know He is sovereign. No event is beyond His control; nothing happens to us by chance. Thus, we can live each day assured God cares about our daily trials and concerns. And we can face the future and press on, knowing our Lord never will stop caring. By faith in His character, we can rely on God through the most difficult times.

Those difficult times will come, too. Rather than putting us on "Easy Street," the life of faith seems to direct us down "Trial Avenue." Not only do we still have questions and problems, but we face new mysteries that not even Sherlock Holmes could begin to solve. We also encounter roadblocks, potholes, and various circumstances that test our confidence in God. We are tempted to give up, to disobey, to trust in something more tangible. Yet we know God's Word urges us to move ahead, to obey our Lord, to trust in the only one who is reliable and infallible. We also know that if we continue on through the tough times we will find that our faith is real and, in fact, has grown stronger.

By faith, we accept the circumstances God gives us in life. By faith, we also accept and obey His Word, even when we do not like what it says or when we do not understand the purpose for a particular command. Like Noah, who was instructed to build an ark for a flood without ever having seen rain, we follow God's command. We trust that the God who created the universe, including us, and who knows the number of hairs on our head, knows what is best and how we should live.

Jesus' life on earth clearly illustrates this life of faith. He demonstrated implicit trust in His Heavenly Father by submitting to His plan. He knew that the Father was in control as He was conceived by the Holy Spirit, born and raised by human parents, tempted, rejected, betrayed, ridiculed, scourged, and crucified. His submission to the Father exemplifies the life of faith, which has been explained as "being open to the possibilities that God presents."[3]

As followers of Christ, are we "open to the possibilities that God presents," including the possibility of children? By faith will we accept our family as something built by God? Will we join the psalmist in proclaiming, "Behold, children are a gift of the LORD; the fruit of the womb is a reward . . . How blessed is the man whose quiver is full of them" (Psalm 127:3, 5)?

Again, we must remember that God has called us to live by faith, and "without faith it is impossible to please Him" (Hebrews 11:6). Thus, by faith we are to accept the children He gives us as gifts, not as threats. And we should trust in His timing. In His sovereign wisdom and abundant love, He will give us children if and when He chooses. We also must entrust ourselves to Him as He uses those children to discipline us, to conform us to the image of His Son. We must see children, and all of life, through the eyes of faith. As we do, we also will see the Biblical ideal for contraception.

CHAPTER 6

THE BIBLICAL IDEAL FOR CONTRACEPTION

Remember Carl and Sue, the engaged couple we met in Chapter 1? What if, instead of abandoning their search for the truth, they turned to the source of truth? Suppose that, as we have done, they examined the Scriptures to see what God says about the morality of contraception. What would they conclude?

Let's find out. Let's join this couple now as they summarize their findings and arrive at the Biblical ideal for contraception.

"No doubt about it." Carl sets his Bible on the table. "Bearing children is one of God's primary purposes for marriage and sex."

"Yes, and it's clear that our relationship is for His glory, not for our benefit." Sue smiles. "Of course I'm glad He's designed it so that as we follow His plan we *will* benefit."

Carl smiles back. "Me too. But you're right. It is important for us to keep our marriage God-centered, not us-centered."

"We also need to keep His perspective on children. Already, as I've seen them as gifts—not burdens, I've gotten more excited about our future 'blessings.' I hope He gives us some!"

"It's reassuring that God directs if and when we'll have children, and how many," Carl says. "After all, our Heavenly Father knows best."

"He certainly does. And He knows best what I should be doing as a wife. He has given me quite a responsibility—taking care of our home and children. What greater contribution to our society could I possibly make? I enjoy my job downtown, but I can see it doesn't begin to compare with the rewards of shaping and molding the lives God gives to us."

"I know God will use our children to shape and mold us too. And hasn't that always been our prayer—that He will conform us to the image of Christ?"

"Yes," Sue agrees. "I guess it would be silly to pray that and then try to stop Him from using children as tools."

"More than that, it would demonstrate a lack of faith. We've seen from the Scripture that we need to trust God in this and in every area of our lives."

They sit quietly for a moment. Then Sue says, "It looks like we have our answer."

Carl nods. "It certainly does. The Biblical ideal for contraception must be that we, or any couple, should not intentionally control conception through *any* means, artificial or 'natural.'"[1]

"In other words, we should have normal, regular

sexual relations without practicing any means of contraception and without being concerned about whether or not I get pregnant."

"That's right. We should fulfill the one-flesh union, leaving the fruit of that union to God. He is the sovereign giver of life, and we should trust Him to give as He sees fit."

"I've heard some people say we should try to have as many children as we can so as to Christianize the world. That's not what this ideal means, is it?"

"No," Carl says. "And it doesn't mean everyone should plan large families. It means we shouldn't plan at all. We should leave the number and timing of children to God—He should be our family planner. Our study of the Scripture has shown that this is His prerogative."

"So, by faith we should allow God to build our family according to His blueprints, rather than trying to build it according to ours," Sue says.

"Exactly. And in light of the character of God, how can we do anything else? Is not our God good?"

"Certainly!"

"Does He not give good gifts?"

"Yes! James 1:17 says, 'Every good thing bestowed and every perfect gift is from above, coming down from the Father of lights, with whom there is no variation, or shifting shadow.'"

"Is our God wise?"

"Of course—the wisest."

"Is He providentially in control?"

"He sure is, and He will accomplish what is best."

"That reminds me of what A. W. Tozer wrote: 'With the goodness of God to desire our highest welfare, the wisdom of God to plan it, and the power of God to achieve it, what do we lack?'"2

"Obviously we lack nothing. In fact, we have all that we need for life. So we can live by faith, trusting in God in all areas of our lives."

"Including the realm of our family," Carl adds.

Sue reflects on their conclusions for a moment. "Does this mean no one should *ever* practice contraception? Is the Biblical ideal *always* ideal for every couple?"

"Good questions. We've seen from God's Word that ideally couples should not practice contraception, but I wonder if there are any exceptions."

"I know how we can find out." Sue picks up Carl's Bible and hands it to him.

Carl smiles. "You're right. It looks like we have some more studying to do!"

PART 3

IS THE IDEAL THE MANDATE?

CHAPTER 7

ARE THERE EXCEPTIONS?

"*I* before *e*, except after *c* and in *neighbor* and *weigh*."
"Yes, this specially priced refrigerator is available in
all colors . . . except white, almond, or gold." "Everybody's
out of step except my Johnny." "We're open 10 to 9 every
day, except Sundays, holidays, and the opening day of
fishing season." "These pants are only $25 . . . except in
your size."

It is difficult to go through a day without running
into exceptions. Life is filled with them. Even when they
try to hide in the fine print, we know they are there. In
fact, sometimes the exceptions seem to outnumber the
rules.

What about in the area of contraception? We have
seen that a primary purpose of marriage and sex is procreation. Our study also revealed that children are gifts
from God, given according to His sovereignty, and that a
wife's role centers on her family and home. And we determined that life is not only a gift, it is a discipline, and it is
to be lived by faith in our trustworthy God. Thus, we con-

cluded, the Biblical ideal is that husbands and wives should not try to prevent conception.

But now we must consider, are there any exceptions to this ideal? Does anything in Scripture indicate that some couples should remain childless, or limit their family size, or control the spacing of their children? Do husbands and wives have any God-given responsibility in this area?

Such questions cannot be answered hastily. We need to again explore the greatest source of truth: God's Word. We also must be careful not to discount *His* role in this and in all areas of life. With this in mind, we will turn to the Bible to see if it allows for exceptions to God's ideal.

Life in a Fallen World

In our examination of contraception we have talked of the Biblical ideal—God's original intent. We saw that He commanded sinless Adam and Eve to reproduce. But Adam and Eve did not remain sinless. And as a result of this disobedience, sin entered all of God's perfect creation. "Therefore, just as through one man sin entered into the world, and death through sin, and so death spread to all men, because all sinned . . ." (Romans 5:12).

Consequently, the world became far less than ideal. "For the creation was subjected to futility, not of its own will, but because of Him who subjected it, in hope that the creation itself also will be set free from its slavery to corruption into the freedom of the glory of the children of God. For we know that the whole creation groans and suffers the pains of childbirth together until now" (Romans 8:20-22).

This less-than-ideal state of the world raises a question. Did the Genesis 1:28 command to "Be fruitful and multiply," which was given before the Fall, lose its validity as a result of the Fall? Didn't God need to change the creation mandates after sin changed the world? Clearly He did not. In Genesis 9:1, 7 He gave the same command to "Be fruitful and multiply" to Noah and his sons, who were born with a sinful nature. From this passage and the other Scriptures regarding marriage we examined in Part 2, it is evident that procreation remains God's will. That has not changed.

This does not mean Adam and Eve's disobedience had no effect on bearing children. According to Scripture—and the convincing testimony of mothers—the entrance of sin caused a tremendous increase in the pain of childbirth (Genesis 3:16). Yet, just as man was cursed with much toil in his work but must still work, couples must still carry out their obligation to be fruitful and multiply.

> The fall did bring revolutionary changes into man's life; yet these ordinances are still in effect and they indicate that the interests and occupations which lay closest to man's heart in original integrity must still lie close to his heart in his fallen state.[1]

Indeed, God's Kingdom program from Genesis 3 onward is designed to reverse the curse, to bring God's ideals into complete realization once more. Even now, those who have been transferred "to the kingdom of His beloved Son" (Colossians 1:13) are part of this new creation.

So the Fall has not eliminated God's commands. It has, however, created a tension between the ideal and its realization. We need only read the Bible and look at ourselves, at others, and at the world to see that God's ideals—the ways He wants things to be—continually are being frustrated. Some frustrations of God's desires result from man's continual sin and rebellion. Others result from living in a fallen world, where death reigns and futility is part of the fabric of life.

These frustrations clearly extend to the arenas of marriage and the family. For example, God created marriage as a bond that was not to be broken. In Deuteronomy 24 and Matthew 19, however, we see allowances for divorce. Jesus explained, "Because of your hardness of heart, Moses permitted you to divorce your wives; but from the beginning it has not been this way" (Matthew 19:8).

Similarly, the Fall apparently allows for the less-than-ideal in the area of contraception. The mandate to reproduce "is confronted with concrete situations which resist its realization and *can* alter it in its application to concrete circumstances."[2] In other words, in certain situations couples may be unable to comply with the ideal. The Fall opens the door to exceptions to God's ideal, to the possibility of controlling conception.

We must not, however, eagerly charge through that door. True, the world is cursed, but the reversal of that curse has begun through Christ's redemptive work on the cross. Even though we will not see the full reversal until the Lord's Second Coming, we are to live in light of our present in-Christ reality. Just as Jesus told His followers to return to the ideal regarding marriage (Mark 10:2-12), believers also should seek the ideal in the area of procreation. The Fall may hinder us in reaching it, but we should aim toward that goal.

In addition, we must remain aware of the control mentality which may influence, however subtly, our decision-making process. This awareness should make us hesitant to even think of modifying God's ideal. Human nature tempts us to grab for possible mitigating factors as the rule rather than as the exception. We tend to look for the easy, convenient way out, in the name of "being Biblical." (For example, the "exception clause" of Matthew 5:32 and 19:9 is often used to justify divorce.) As believers, however, we must be vigilant to seek God's will and to not be conformed to the world.

But, again, there are tensions. How do we know if our circumstance is a legitimate barrier to procreation? How do we discern if and when God would have us take exception to His ideal and practice contraception? In succeeding chapters, we will consider concrete situations that might merit taking exception. But first, to help us answer these questions and evaluate such situations, we will look at four guiding principles from Scripture.

1) Life Is a Stewardship

In the beginning of time, God appointed men and women as stewards of life. He gave us dominion over creation.

> And God created man in His own
> image . . . male and female He created
> them. And God blessed them; and God
> said to them, "Be fruitful and multiply,
> and fill the earth, and subdue it; and
> rule over the fish of the sea and over
> the birds of the sky, and over every liv-
> ing thing that moves on the earth."
> (Genesis 1:27, 28)

David, in awe of the Creator and Lord, and in wonder at the place of authority He has given man, wrote:

> You made him ruler over the works of
> Your hands; you put everything under
> his feet: all flocks and herds, and the
> beasts of the field, the birds of the air,
> and the fish of the sea, all that swim
> the paths of the seas. (Psalm 8:6-8,
> NIV).

Since God has given us dominion over creation,
does that mean He has given us dominion over procreation? Some Christians would say yes. They conclude
that controlling conception is among our responsibilities
as stewards of His creation. Just as we must be responsible in the use of our God-given natural resources, we
must be responsible in the use of our God-given repro-
ductive power. It is our duty, they believe.

But is this true? Does man's dominion over creation automatically give him the right to limit conception? Is that included in the nature and scope of his rule? In answering these questions, we must first examine what it means to "rule."

In the Old Testament, "have dominion" or "rule" (*rada*) often is used to describe a king's rule over his subjects. Solomon wrote, "May he [the king] also rule from sea to sea, and from the river to the ends of the earth" (Psalm 72:8). This rule is not merely a position and privilege; it is a responsibility to maintain righteousness and to observe God's Laws.

> And the king went up to the house of the LORD and all the men of Judah and all the inhabitants of Jerusalem with him, and the priests and the prophets and all the people . . . and he read in their hearing all the words of the book of the covenant. . . . And the king . . . made a covenant before the LORD, to walk after the LORD, and to keep His commandments and His testimonies and His statutes with all his heart and all his soul. (2 Kings 23:2, 3)

The king also is expected to care for those he governs. God rebukes those self-serving rulers who take wonderful care of themselves while they neglect the sick, broken, scattered, and lost, and who dominate their subjects "with force and with severity" (Ezekiel 34:2-4). In ruling, man is to serve God's interests, not his own.

From the use of "rule" in Scripture, we learn that those who reign over others do not reign over themselves. They are under the rule and authority of God. King David recognized this truth. Throughout the Psalms he sought God's favor and praised God's graciousness. He knew that "The LORD will accomplish what concerns me" (Psalm 138:8). As king over Israel, he acknowledged that God was King over all—including the king of Israel.

> King David went in and sat before the LORD, and he said: "Who am I, O Sovereign LORD, and what is my family, that you have brought me this far? . . . O Sovereign LORD, you have also spoken about the future of the house of your servant. . . . For the sake of your word and according to your will, you have done this great thing and made it known to your servant." (2 Samuel 7:18, 19, 21, NIV)

From these and other passages, we can see that God has granted to man dominion, but not His sovereignty. God remains in control. As an apartment owner gives another the responsibility to manage his property, God has given us stewardship of some of His possessions. We must remember that while we have responsibility over those areas, we do not have ownership or ultimate authority.

But which aspects of His creation has the Creator put in our charge? Do we have dominion over all things, or has God given our realm parameters? If the latter, what are they?

We already have determined that man's realm lies within the limits of God's sovereignty. We are to rule under God, cooperating with and depending on Him, promoting His ends by His means. But that still does not define our boundaries. Specifically, it does not answer the question, Does man's dominion extend to himself, and thus give him the right and responsibility to control conception?

Before we answer, we must consider a warning:

> We must be careful to ensure in an effort to define limits of dominion we do not confine ourselves so much that we oppose all human endeavors for improvement. In our reverence for God and in our desire to do His will, it is possible to interpret all reality as the expression of God's perfect will. Such a position would remove us from the realm of being responsible creatures and, in practical terms, force us to renounce all medicine, mechanical assists, and so forth.[3]

To avoid confining ourselves needlessly or trying to rule beyond our parameters, we must look for God's definition of our stewardship. In doing so, we need not look far. At Creation God said we are to rule over the fish, the birds, the cattle, and every creeping thing (Genesis 1:26-28). Likewise, Psalm 8 lists flocks, herds, beasts, birds, and fish as the works in our domain. God also has given us "every plant yielding seed . . . and every tree which has fruit yielding seed" (Genesis 1:29).

As important as noting what is included in our domain is to note what is excluded: man himself. Though he is to care for himself, man is not king over himself. Rather, as Francis Schaeffer pointed out, "Man has dominion over the 'lower' orders of creation."[4] God clearly has dominion over man.

What does all this mean in our consideration of this guiding principle for exceptions? It means we can conclude that our dominion *in and of itself* does not give us the right and responsibility to control conception. God has not included that in our realm. Because of the tension caused by the Fall, however, under certain conditions it *may* be impossible to maintain the Biblical ideal of procreation while exercising good stewardship over His creation. In some cases it may be necessary to practice contraception in order to love God and our fellowman and to demonstrate the sacredness and value of human life.

2) The Concerns of the Kingdom Are Paramount

The Kingdom of God is at hand. Throughout the New Testament we are admonished to keep that fact in the forefront of our minds and hearts. The imminence of the

Kingdom is to affect our behavior and decisions—even the decision of whether or not to marry. Jesus spoke of "eunuchs who made themselves eunuchs for the sake of the kingdom of heaven" (Matthew 19:12). Paul advised the unmarried to consider remaining single in light of the distress and urgency facing Christians. He wrote, "One who is unmarried is concerned about the things of the Lord, how he may please the Lord; but one who is married is concerned about the things of the world, how he may please his wife, and his interests are divided" (1 Corinthians 7:32-34).

If having a spouse distracts us from the Lord's work, how much more does having children! And since Scripture allows Christians to choose celibacy for the sake of the Kingdom, surely Christian couples can choose to remain childless for that same reason. Or so it might appear.

But is this conclusion valid? In Matthew 19 and 1 Corinthians 7, the issue is marriage versus celibacy. Paul makes numerous points for the latter, since marriage carries with it additional burdens and concerns. Marriage is thus presented as a tougher course of life than celibacy. It also is presented as optional. Nowhere in Scripture, however, do we find that procreation within marriage is optional. Nor do we find anywhere in Scripture that we should limit the number of children.

In Paul's letter to the Corinthians, as well as in his other epistles, his focus on the heavenly dimension of God's Kingdom does not discount earthly relationships. Rather, the heavenly perspective helps believers see and experience marriage as the holy bond God intended. For example, in Ephesians 5 the exaltation of Christ exalts marriage as a depiction of the union of the Bridegroom with the church. In Colossians the apostle says to "Set your mind on the things above" (3:2) and therefore put aside sinful living and put on Christlike qualities in your human relationships—including your relationships with your spouse and children.

Paul's teaching also brings to light the tension we experience as Christians. Yes, the new world has begun, but it has begun here, in this old fallen world. We are to hope in and live for the Lord's return, yet we also are to live out our earthly relationships. We have seen that if we are married, a God-ordained aspect of that relationship is childbearing (unless God closes the wife's womb). Certainly caring for those children, as well as being married, takes time and energy, but neither necessarily prevents us from serving our King. Rather, nurturing our children with Christian love and instruction is an important part of our work for God's Kingdom. *They* are our most important disciples.

Therefore, while the imminence of the Kingdom should affect how we live, it does not *in and of itself* affect the Biblical ideal regarding contraception. Because our world is cursed, however, it might. It *could* be necessary for a couple to control conception for some higher moral purpose relating to advancing God's Kingdom, for some common commitment to a specific God-given calling.[5]

Again, this principle would cause only certain couples in certain situations to take exception to the Biblical ideal. Even so, we should be very careful about making such exceptions because it is all too easy to make exceptions for the wrong reasons. As we have seen from Scripture, childbearing is a God-given, and thus God-glorifying, role for most husbands and wives. It is a vital part of their ministry, not a hindrance to it.

3) The Purposes of Marriage and Sex May Need to Be Balanced

As we saw in Chapter 3, Scripture teaches that marriage and sex have two purposes: procreation and the one-flesh unity between husband and wife. These two purposes are complementary, not competitive. Children vividly illustrate, rather than prevent, the one-flesh union. Thus we generally need not choose between fulfilling one purpose or the other. Most married couples can fulfill them both simultaneously. That clearly is God's intent.

Yet, again we face a tension between the ideal and reality as a result of sin's presence in our world.

> Since the Fall, in this aeon of "hard-heartedness," it is possible for two integral elements of the order of creation to come into conflict with each other. In other words, there can be a conflict between the oneness of wedlock and parenthood on the one hand, and responsibility to procreate life on the other. In the unbroken world as it

was in its original state . . . it was *not*
so. There the intention of creation and
responsibility still coincided.[6]

Because we are sinful creatures living in a sinful world, a couple *may* need to try to prevent conception for the sake of their marital unity. In some situations a husband and wife *may* need to focus on their relationship before they fulfill the purpose of procreation. When their unity is restored, however, they should stop practicing contraception so they can then, Lord willing, fulfill the other purpose of their marriage.

4) Parents Are Responsible to Provide for the Needs of Their Children

The Bible clearly teaches that parents are to care for their children. This means providing for their spiritual needs as well as their physical needs. Parents are told to "Train up a child in the way he should go" (Proverbs 22:6), to "bring them up in the discipline and instruction of the Lord" (Ephesians 6:4). Mothers and fathers are to nurture their children in the fullness of the Christian faith.

Because of the Fall, a husband and wife *may* experience a tension between following the Biblical ideal and following this principle. At least temporarily, they may not be able to bear children and care for them properly. As responsible believers, they *may* need to practice contraception until they are able to provide for their children as God intends.

Physical limitations may possibly enter in as well.

For example, a wife may have some serious physical complication whereby pregnancy would threaten her life. The couple *may* need to practice contraception in such an instance. More will be presented on this issue in the next chapter.

The Overriding Guiding Principle

These four principles may lead a couple to control conception, at least for a time and to a degree. We must not grab at these, however, and take them as the rule. Just as we are not to use Matthew 5:32 or 19:9 as an escape clause from our marriage commitments, we must not use these principles to avoid our God-given responsibility of parenthood. They should be considered only by couples who are honestly seeking the will of God in this matter—not by those who are seeking to disguise their rebellion against God's will.

That brings us to the overriding principle regarding exceptions. Because of the presence of sin in our world, in a specific mandated situation conception may need to be controlled for the good of the individual, the family, or society—good as defined by God and Scripture. "For the good" means the husband and wife are acting in love, not selfishness. They are seeking God's interests, not their own.

Exceptions to the Biblical ideal, however, must never be taken lightly. Nor are they to be taken eagerly, with a sigh of relief. Rather, any situation leading us to consider limiting our family must be weighed carefully. We must evaluate the circumstances, as well our hearts, before the Lord. And any exception must always be viewed as an exception, never as the rule. In other words, the concrete situation must never be made "the standard of judgment and thus pragmatically distort the order of creation, but rather . . . [it must be] exercised only under the claim and under the judgment of the order of creation."[7]

Because such a situation is the exception, we must not limit conception without being firmly convinced before God that it is for His and our best. We must have sufficient cause—an undeniably strong case—as "the burden of proof rests squarely upon those who would control the gift of the Author and Giver of life—this life that is a standing rebuke to death and is fit to be redeemed from the curse of death. . . ."[8] Before making our decision, we must seek God's wisdom through the study and *accurate* application of His Word and through much prayer.[9]

As we strive to discern God's will, we also must examine our motives. Are they God-centered or self-centered? Are we truly seeking to glorify God? With these questions in mind, we now will evaluate several potential social and personal motives for practicing contraception.

CHAPTER 8

SOCIAL MOTIVES FOR CONTRACEPTION

When you were young, you learned a powerful three-letter word. It was powerful not only because its repeated use gradually altered your parents' facial expression and vocal tone (although those results could not be ignored). No, the true strength of your word was in its ability to open up the world before you. By asking, "Why?" you could learn about the nature of creation—why birds flew away in the winter, why the leaves fell off the trees in the fall, why the seeds you planted grew into carrots, and why you needed to leave the carrots in the ground until they finished growing (rather than pulling them up daily to check their progress).

By asking, "Why?" you also learned about the nature of people—why Dad went to work every morning, why Mom made you drink your milk, why your big brother would not let you play with his model airplane. Sometimes you didn't like the answers you received, but whether or not you realized it, you learned from them.

Such questions were a vital part of early education, for all of us.

As adults, however, we too seldom ask, "Why?" Perhaps it is because we remember disappointing responses we received as children. Or, since our parents tired of our ceaseless inquisitiveness, we assume our questions are never appropriate. Most likely, though, we neglect to use that potent three-letter word because we forget or because we are lazy. Now that we are expected to answer our own questions, it is easier not to ask.

Yet, if we are going to take exception to God's ideal, we need to ask, "Why?" We cannot practice contraception "just because." We need a strong, Scriptural reason resulting from much prayer and a wholehearted desire to follow God's leading. The distressing thing is that when we are speaking of contraception, we are usually speaking of "a practice already engaged in by many Christians who have seldom reckoned seriously with the bearing of the biblical teaching upon that practice."[1]

Over the centuries when people have asked or been asked, "Why?" they have cited similar motives for practicing contraception. Unmarried women wish to prevent pregnancy; people worry about the earth's growing population; married couples wish to avoid having children for health or economic reasons.[2] The repeated use of these motives, however, does not justify them. How often have people stayed home from work because they had a more desirable option? Does that make it a legitimate motive?

The only true standard for evaluating motives is

God's Word. So that is what we now will do. In this chapter and the next, we will analyze these common social and personal motives in light of the Biblical ideal and the guiding principles we discussed in Chapter 7.

Avoiding the Fruit of Sin

"Do not be deceived, God is not mocked; for whatever a man sows, this he will also reap" (Galatians 6:7). Just ask David. He seemed to think he could get away with a little sin, a little adultery. Then Bathsheba dropped the bombshell: "I am pregnant" (2 Samuel 11:5). His one-night stand turned into a lifelong nightmare (2 Samuel 12:10, 11).

David's example reinforces for all of us the fact that sin has consequences. It causes problems in our lives and, most importantly, grieves our Lord. The only way to avoid these results is to avoid sin.

Some people, however, would rather continue to sin, but try to avoid its consequences. Thieves wear masks and work at night so they won't be seen. Businessmen destroy or doctor incriminating documents. Unmarried lovers use birth control.

Obviously, as believers we immediately can dismiss this motive for practicing contraception. Scripture clearly teaches that sex is good—between a husband and wife. From Genesis 2:24 onward, we see that God intends for this gift to be confined to the marriage relationship.

We also find that violating God's will for sexual intercourse incurs a strict penalty. Fornicators and adulterers, as well as idolaters, head Paul's list of those who will not inherit the Kingdom of God (1 Corinthians 6:9, 10). He also includes homosexuals, thieves, drunkards, and swindlers. Likewise, when Paul contrasts the deeds of the flesh with the fruit of the Spirit, he begins the first list with sexual immorality. It is followed by "impurity, sensuality, idolatry, sorcery, enmities, strife, jealousy, outbursts of anger, disputes, dissensions, factions, envyings, drunkenness, carousings, and things like these, of which I forewarn you just as I have forewarned you that those who practice such things shall not inherit the kingdom of God" (Galatians 5:19-21).

There is no question about it: God does not approve of premarital and extramarital intercourse. They are sin. They also are the "denial of one of the essential purposes of sexuality, namely, a personal relationship designed to be permanent and the willingness to accept the office of parenthood."[3] Fornication and adultery are not valid options for Christians. Thus, it is not legitimate for believers to practice contraception to avoid a pregnancy that might result from these immoral relationships. This clearly is not a valid, God-centered motive.

Slowing the Growing Population

In 1650 the world population was 470 million. By the start of 1986, it had grown about ten times larger, to nearly 4.5 billion. People are alarmed. For many people, overpopulation is seen as the root of most of the world's problems, the cancer inflicting our planet.[4] But how accurate is this? Does the issue of population truly give "burden of proof" to go against God's ideal and allow contraception?

After studying the issue, economics professor J. R.

Kasun concluded that "the so-called 'population crisis' is more truly a myth and an alibi than a fact."[5] Others agree. In fact, many say that population growth is in reality good for humanity. Let's pursue this further.

Some have argued that the increased population is causing numerous problems. Food shortages, pollution, environmental destruction, and other ecological concerns seem to point to the need for contraception. But is that truly where the blame lies? Is overpopulation the real culprit in these concerns?

Let's examine the population's relationship to the food shortage. Obviously the more people we have, the more food we need. And since each day people die of starvation, we apparently do not have enough food. Therefore, it follows that if people had fewer children, we would have enough food to go around.

This sounds like good logic, but in reality these are myths.[6] We *do* have enough food already, and more can be grown! As noted by Kasun in her recent book *The War Against Population*, "world food output has continued to match or outstrip population growth."[7] Others concur:[8]

> . . . there ought to be sufficient food both now and in the future. . . .

> Food production in the world is now increasing much faster than the population. . . .

> Because large sections of the world,

especially in the developing areas, appear crowded and on the verge of famine, most observers seem to feel that the gap between food demand and food supply must inevitably grow. But we argue that, as a direct consequence of available resources and improving technology, a more reasonable projection would be in the direction of an eventual abundance of food....

. . . this earth is already producing enough food to feed more than 6 billion people—hundreds of millions more than are now alive.

Yes, people are starving, but it is not because we have too many people and too little food. It is because too few people have access to the available food. As one expert writes, "The problem now is not lack of production, but lack of rational distribution and even destruction of food surpluses."[9]

This was evident in 1984 when Ethiopian drought victims needlessly died of starvation. People from the Western world sent generous contributions of food supplies, but Ethiopia's ports were equipped to receive only a limited amount each month. Once the food arrived, distribution was hindered by the rough mountain terrain leading to the majority of villages and, most disturbingly, by the interference of the Communist government and rebel factions.[10]

Even in our own cities one man goes to bed hungry, while his neighbor moans from overindulgence. One woman savors a piece of stale bread, while another throws out leftover roast beef. Again we see that the distribution, rather than the quantity, of food is the problem.

The blame for hunger in our world lies not with the number of people. Indeed, it does not really lie in the lack of distribution of resources or in their destruction per se. At its core the blame must lie with political ideologies and systems, moral values and choices, greed and selfish ambition. Hunger is due to the attitudes and actions of sinful man, not to the appetites of large families. This was all too evident in the situation in Ethiopia:

> The elements in the little publicized
> side of Ethiopia's famine—civil war, a
> brutal Marxist regime, forced resettle-
> ments, and food seized by the govern-
> ment—cause more misery than
> overpopulation, or in Ethiopia's case,
> the well-publicized drought.[11]

What about ecological problems? Again, these stem not from the change in population size, but from the change in attitudes and values. The effect of these values also has left its mark. "At the root of the ecological crisis is human greed, what has been called 'economic gain by environmental loss.'"[12] Yet, rather than stop the exploitation of their land, we distribute contraceptive devices. We try to decrease the number of mouths the deteriorating land must support. This does not solve the problem; it only soothes our consciences.

While we can perhaps say that some parts of the world have more people than resources available to meet their needs, we cannot blame the imbalance on the number of people. It is values—not numbers—that have caused the environment to lose its resiliency. Overdevelopment, overcultivation, overgrazing, deforestation, and other actions that lead to environmental destruction and disasters result from overindulgence rather than overpopulation.

Then how do we restore the balance of nature? Clearly, the key is in stopping man's exploitation of the environment. We must "repent of extravagance, pollution, and wanton destruction."[13] We must deal with the problem at its roots, by changing the way we think and live.

The true problem, then, is sinful humanity. As a result, there are wrong worldviews, destructive pagan values, etc., which lead to actions and attitudes which cause the surface problems of poverty and hunger, dilemmas many want to blame on overpopulation.[14] Note the following excerpts from the 1977 *Villars Statement on Relief and Development*:[15]

> The devastating reality of sin and evil
> (hunger, oppression, deprivation, dis-

ease, death, and separation from God) is the result of man's rebellion against God, which began at the Fall and continues through history.

The causes of hunger and deprivations, therefore, are spiritual as well as material and can only be dealt with adequately insofar as the spiritual dimension is taken into account.

Man's rebellion against God affects every aspect of human existence. The Fall resulted in God's curse on creation and in destructive patterns of thought, culture, and relationships, which keep men and women in bondage to poverty and deprivation.

The work of Christian relief and development, therefore, must involve spiritual transformation, setting people free from destructive attitudes, beliefs, values, and patterns of culture.

In conclusion, overpopulation is not to blame for our world's problems. In fact, overpopulation as a root cause is a myth. There is no crisis of population in most cases. Overpopulation is *not* leading to less food, nor to ecological problems. Nor does it lead to an exhaustion of resources,[16] to "running out of space,"[17] or to unemployment in the long run.[18] Indeed, population increase may very well be good for mankind[19]—which, of course, corresponds to the Lord's own mandate to "Be fruitful and multiply" (Genesis 1:28).

But even for those who think there is some cause for concern, the solution is not contraception—just as abortion, euthanasia, and genocide are not the answer.[20] As Mother Teresa commented: "Why are people so worried about world population? There is plenty of land in India for people to live on. It is so rich a country. . . . Children should be a joy and a pleasure."[21] We may genuinely be concerned about the welfare of mankind, but the end never justifies the means. The means, in and of themselves, must be justifiable.

Finally, we also must remember that contraception must remain a theological, not a biological or social, issue. Our evaluations of motives must be based on Scripture, and our actions must be in faith and for the glory of God.[22] This holds true whether we are considering the welfare of our world or the welfare of our family. And we must keep this in mind as we now turn to this latter motive for controlling conception.

CHAPTER 9

PERSONAL MOTIVES FOR CONTRACEPTION

Have you ever been gathered together with other believers and run out of things to talk about? You've more than adequately covered the weather, the playoffs, the housing market, and the latest department store sales. You've even expressed your concern about crime rates, social reform, and teenage hairstyles. Now the silence weighs heavy on you.

Next time you find yourself in such a situation, liven up the conversation by asking, "Do you think Christian couples should practice contraception?" Some may blush, others may leave, but some may answer. If they say, "Yes," ask them why.

You probably will find, as I have, that no one will say, "So partners can engage in immorality without getting pregnant." Nor should you expect to hear, "Because the world is overpopulated." Rather, most answers will center on the welfare of the family—concerns about physical and emotional health, finances, and other personal issues. So we now will consider these motives.

Protecting the Wife's Health

One common motive for practicing contraception is the physical well-being of the potential mother. Some couples want to guard the woman's health by ensuring she has sufficient time between pregnancies. Others see childbirth as a risk due to specific physical problems or the wife's age.

Throughout the centuries, this motive generally has been accepted. *The Talmud*, which contained the Jewish civil and religious law, made some allowance for contraception when the woman's health was endangered.[1] More recently, Karl Menninger commented:

> There are certainly some women who are well enough to have sexual intercourse but not well enough to bear children, and it would seem to me that the health of such women should be safeguarded without forcing them to be continent and without forcing their husbands to choose between continence and adultery.[2]

In our fallen world, it seems that physical danger to the wife could provide sufficient reason for a couple to take exception to the Biblical ideal. Before reaching this decision, however, the couple should ask two questions: Is the wife's health truly in danger? And is this the couple's true motive, or is it a convenient rationale that masks more self-centered reasons? Before choosing to practice contraception, the couple must honestly answer these questions before the Lord.

In considering this motive, we also must not overlook that a wife's health may be endangered by *not* having children. Medical findings indicate that breast cancer, as well as menstrual difficulties, may be due to the physical stress caused by years of repeated menstrual cycles without fertilization. Cancer of the ovaries and uterine lining also seem to be more prevalent in women who never have given birth, presumably because they ovulate each month for most of their adult life.[3]

While more research is needed, we cannot ignore the medical evidence pointing to these risks of remaining childless. We also cannot deny that virtually all common artificial contraception devices pose health hazards for their users. Thus, following the Biblical ideal may prove most beneficial for the wife's health.

If particular medical concerns outweigh these dangers, however, the couple may have a legitimate reason to limit conception. Such a couple faces a difficult decision. They must come to their conclusion carefully and prayerfully, seeking God's will and glory.

Preventing the Transmission of Diseases or Defects

Another dilemma arises when a couple is likely to produce an infant with inheritable and incurable physical or mental defects. Many would say such a couple not only can legitimately practice contraception, but *must*. It is their responsibility, as children have a right to be born relatively healthy. Knowingly bearing an unhealthy child is immoral, some argue, and puts an unnecessary burden on the society that will need to care for him or her.[4]

While these circumstances may indeed be grounds for departing from the Biblical ideal, the diversion must not be automatic. Again, the husband and wife must search their hearts before the Lord and ask difficult questions.

First, they must consider, is not God sovereign in the formation of each person? As David wrote, "For Thou didst form my inward parts; Thou didst weave me in my mother's womb" (Psalm 139:13). And in Exodus 4:11 God told Moses, "Who has made man's mouth? Or who makes him dumb or deaf, or seeing or blind? Is it not I, the LORD?"

God is in providential control of all conceptions, and if a child has inherited defects, God is not caught by surprise. Our Creator and Lord knew long before the parents or doctor. He also knows whether that child should be born or should be naturally miscarried. As evidence of God's sovereign wisdom and mercy, approximately 80 percent of all miscarried fetuses have a serious defect or deformity.

This does not diminish the suffering of a miscarriage or of bearing an unhealthy child. Nor should God's sovereignty over defects and diseases lead us to conclude that such problems should never be treated. But it should remind us that we can trust our Lord in this and all areas of life.

Second, a couple considering contraception for this reason must ask if the quality-of-life ethic is valid. If so, who determines the acceptable level of quality?

If we accept this ethic, it implies we think only a normal life has value. An abnormal life, then, is less valuable than no life at all. Yet, this reasoning has been shown to be false. "A well documented investigation has shown that there is no difference between malformed and normal persons in their degree of life satisfaction, outlook on what lies immediately ahead, and vulnerability to frustration."[5]

In Scripture we also see that all life has value and that defects can have a specific purpose. Jesus pointed this out to His disciples when they questioned Him about a blind man. "His disciples asked Him, saying, 'Rabbi, who sinned, this man, or his parents, that he should be born blind?' Jesus answered, 'It was neither that this man sinned, nor his parents; but it was in order that the works of God might be displayed in him'" (John 9:2, 3).

This brings us to our third question. What about the value of the "abnormal" child in the parents' lives? In Chapter 5 we saw that life is a discipline; that God uses children to help conform us to the image of Christ. It is possible that the lessons He has for some of us can be taught only through the blessing of a less-than-healthy child. Should we, the clay, try to stop the potter from using these necessary tools to mold us?

As we consider this issue, we must keep an eternal perspective. Parents of unhealthy children, as well as the children themselves, might suffer in this world, but that suffering certainly is worth the rewards they will receive in Heaven. To confirm this hope we need only look to "Jesus, the author and perfecter of faith, who for the joy set before Him endured the cross, despising the shame, and has sat down at the right hand of the throne of God" (Hebrews 12:2). Clearly, our eternal reward makes any temporary suffering worthwhile.

Fourth, husbands and wives need to ask if their motive for practicing contraception is to prevent suffering or to perform selective breeding. Earlier we concluded that God does not intend for us to exercise that power. We must not use contraception to control the future generation—to make it what we want it to be, for whatever reasons.

After carefully considering these questions, the couple must decide if the risk of transmitting a disease is sufficient cause for practicing contraception. They must decide before the Lord if they should take exception to the Biblical ideal by trying to prevent children from being born into their marriage.

Finally, since a primary purpose for marriage is procreation, should men and women with inheritable diseases wed if they believe they should not have children? This, too, is a difficult question. But after prayerfully seeking an answer, they may decide His will for them is celibacy. "A person who knows he (or she) carries a defect or a disease which is transmissible to the children he (or she) may have should be prepared to forgo, in the interests both of the family and of the race, the privilege and the pleasure of marriage and parenthood."[6]

Ensuring the Ability to Provide

A mother saw her three-year-old son swallow a nickel. She rushed over and grabbed the boy, turned him upside-down, and sharply hit his back. As she did, he coughed up two dimes. The woman was beside herself! She ran to the door and cried out to her husband, "Johnny just swallowed a nickel and then coughed up two dimes. What should I do?"

The father yelled back, "Keep feeding him nickels!"[7]

Don't we sometimes wish it were that easy? Perhaps we even have dreamed of our child making a small (or large) fortune by starring in television commercials. It's not that we don't appreciate the joy and nonmaterial rewards he or she brings; it's just that we would not mind a little help paying the bills.

Yet, deep down we know that while children are a reward, they also are an expense. For some husbands and wives, this is a primary consideration in their decision about practicing contraception. They want to ensure they can reasonably care for each child they bring into this world. Generally these parents already have at least one child and do not believe they can adequately support any more.

Many Christians see this as a legitimate motive for departing from the Biblical ideal. They often appeal to Scripture, citing 1 Timothy 5:8—"But if any one does not provide for his own, and especially for those of his household, he has denied the faith, and is worse than an unbeliever." They believe we should avoid falling into that category by carefully planning. Jesus said, "For which one of you, when he wants to build a tower, does not first sit down and calculate the cost, to see if he has enough to complete it?" (Luke 14:28).

While, as we saw in Chapter 7, in some instances this motive may be valid, this application of these verses is questionable. In 1 Timothy Paul is condemning laziness, not encouraging contraception. He is criticizing those who fail to try to provide for their own. And in Luke, Jesus is speaking of the cost of following Him, of being His disciple. Neither verse is set in the context of bearing children.

Rather than appealing to these Scriptures, then, let us appeal to the character of God. If He chooses to give a husband and wife the gift of a child, will He not also enable them to provide for that child? He who clothes the flowers and feeds the birds certainly will care for the families who trust in Him (Matthew 6).

> Let the fruitful family, however poor, lay this to heart: "Children are an heritage of the Lord: and the fruit of the womb is his reward." And he who gave them will feed them; for it is a fact, and the maxim formed on it has never failed. "Wherever God sends mouths, he sends meat." "Murmur not," said an Arab to his friend, "because thy family is large; know that it is for their sakes that God feeds thee."[8]

Some argue, though, that our world has changed from rural, where large families seemed more fitting, to urban. True, but our God has not changed. Nor has His command to multiply been altered. And while that initial command was given to farmers, most New Testament books, which confirm the couple's responsibility to procreate, were written to city-dwellers. Besides, we cannot assume a husband and wife who follow the Biblical ideal will have a large family. God may give them one child, two, several, or He may give them none. In His wisdom He will populate the quiver, and in His power He will meet their needs.

God may not meet all our wants, however, which leads us to ask, Are we really unable to provide for a child, or do we simply not want to change our lifestyle or standard of living? In a 1982 demographic analysis, researchers at the Rand Corporation concluded that a major factor in our country's decline in fertility is the increase in the employment of women, most of whom work not out of need, but out of an unwillingness to sacrifice income for children.[9] Clearly this is not a Biblically valid reason for preventing or limiting conception.

Nor is it legitimate to practice contraception so we can afford everything we want for the one or two children we have. It is more important that we give them love than their own room complete with telephone, stereo, and television. They need the things money cannot buy.

Of course, children also need food, clothing, and shelter, and some couples may not be equipped to provide those. They may have legitimate financial concerns that would cause them to take exception to the Biblical ideal, at least temporarily. Again, this decision must be based on an inability rather than an unwillingness. And it must be made prayerfully before the Lord.

Meeting the Parents' Personal Needs

While some couples say they practice contraception to protect the wife's health, to prevent the transmission of diseases, or to ensure they can provide for their children, most will give other reasons. These motives fall into the broad category of the husband and wife's psychological and personal needs. Again, these reasons may be valid, but that cannot be decided apart from prayer and the seeking of God's wisdom. Indeed, it is evident that this broad category includes the most reasons which do *not* constitute sufficient "burden of proof" for the practice of contraception. Couples must examine their hearts and the Scriptures before reaching any conclusions. They must carefully consider their motive, which generally will fit into one of the following areas.

First, a couple may desire to prevent conception because the husband or wife has an authentic psychological problem. If they are aware of this problem before walking down the aisle, however, shouldn't they cancel or postpone their wedding rather than getting married and remaining childless? If it is unwise for them to have children, it probably is equally unwise for them to get married.

If a psychological problem arises after marriage, the couple must address and deal with the concern, not simply choose to prevent pregnancy. Remaining childless may be necessary while the problem is being resolved, but it should be viewed as a temporary aid rather than a permanent solution.

Second, many husbands and wives choose to practice contraception so they can become adjusted to each other and to their relationship. It commonly is argued that newlyweds need time to get to know, love, and cherish each other before they take on the responsibility of parenthood. Then, when they feel ready, they can begin their family.

Yet, we must not lose sight of one of God's purposes for marriage: procreation. If a couple is not ready for that responsibility, are they ready for marriage? Perhaps they need to extend their engagement. Also, we must remember God has built into marriage an adjustment period of at least nine months, and usually longer.

A third motive couples give is they are waiting for a more opportune time to have children. One or both partners may be students, and they want to wait until after graduation. Or they may be postponing their family until their income increases, or until they can buy a home. They are delaying until one or more circumstances change.

Parents will testify, however, that there is no such thing as the ideal time for having children. Any couple could find a number of convincing reasons for waiting, but most would be hard-pressed to support them Scripturally. Only in extreme cases is this motive valid. Therefore, rather than waiting for the opportune time, couples should wait on the Lord, trusting in Him. He alone knows the future and will give children in His perfect timing.

Fourth, some couples want to prevent or limit conception because they believe a child would be a burden. We already have seen that in some cases the physical, economic, or emotional strain of having a child may justify a deviation from the Biblical ideal. This motive is not acceptable, however, if the couple simply wants to avoid hassles and sacrifices. We have seen that procreation is a responsibility and life is a discipline to be lived by faith. We also have seen that children are a blessing. Who are we to call these gifts of God a burden?

Fifth, husbands and wives sometimes practice contraception because of their feelings of insecurity. Their self-concept hinges on making a certain amount of money and maintaining a certain standard of living. Thus, they must do what they can, including limit their family, to keep up with the Joneses.

Unless one or both partners has a genuine psychological disorder (in which case they must make efforts to resolve it), this motive has no place in the believer's decision-making process. A Christian's security is in the Lord, not in income or status. Therefore children, who are a gift from that same Lord, cannot be considered a threat to security.

A sixth reason for limiting conception is a fear of pregnancy—a fear that inhibits the enjoyment of the sexual relationship or a fear of having too many children. These concerns boil down to a fear of God. Certainly we can and should trust our living Heavenly Father to give His gifts when and if He chooses. We also must remember He will not necessarily give us an abundance of those gifts. Even in Scripture, the exceptionally large family is just that—an exception. Obviously we cannot know what He will give us, but we can trust Him to give what is best.

Seventh, it is argued that every child has a right to be born planned for, or at least wanted. Therefore, parents practice contraception until they desire a child. If and when that time comes, they try to conceive. Until then, however, they prevent the birth of an unwanted child.

While it is true that no child should be born unwanted, that does not mean a husband and wife should prevent his birth. Rather, they should change their attitude. As Christians, they must reject the prevalent narcissistic control mentality that causes couples to not want children. They must embrace instead the Biblical perspective that bearing children is their responsibility and privilege. For believers, every child should be wanted and received as a precious gift.

One must also ask, Is there for the Christian truly such a thing as an "unwanted" child—i.e., "unwanted" after it has been born? Is not this just another myth we drag into the decision-making process when it comes to thinking of preventing conception? Is it not often true that the "unplanned" child typically is also the cherished child? I know of no Christian couple who would just as soon not have one of their children.

A final motive for controlling conception is to enhance the husband and wife's fulfillment. They want to retain their freedom and mobility and to guard the pleasure of their sexual relationship. Thus they prevent the birth of children, who are inconvenient and can interfere with their parents' personal pursuits. They practice con-traception to protect their own interests.

This motive clearly is unacceptable for Christians. Any reason to depart from the Biblical ideal must be God-centered, not self-centered. Our actions must be for His glory, not for our comfort and pleasure. In addition, we must remember that if we search for fulfillment we never will find it. True fulfillment comes only from following God's plan for our lives.

A Common Thread

Whatever motive couples give for practicing contracep-tion, too often the underlying attitude is, "We have a right to limit conception." They assume the right to protect their physical and psychological well-being, to bear only healthy offspring, to be financially secure, or to pursue personal goals. To ensure those rights, they control the number and spacing of their children.

As we have seen, however, this attitude results not from having the mind of Christ, but from embracing the control mentality of the world.[10] People want rights with-out responsibilities, pleasure and freedom without con-sequences. Yet, as Christians we are called to follow Him who gave up His rights and privileges and thus glorified God by fulfilling His purpose.

As Christians, we also have freedom, don't we? Yes, but Christian freedom is not primarily freedom to use our ratio-nal faculties in decisions. Rather, it is first and foremost freedom to know God, to walk by faith, and to obey Him. Christ did not free us to go our own way, but to go His way.

Thus, couples considering practicing contraception must carefully choose their path. They must ask difficult, penetrating questions. Through careful, Biblical scrutiny they must ascertain whether they are following their personal desires or God's perfect will for them.

In determining God's will, couples must ask Him for wisdom, the Biblical wisdom characterized by obedience and godly fear. They also need to ask themselves whether they have blindly accepted the prevailing notions about marriage and children or have sought to know the mind of God and to base their decision on His Word. They must focus on the character of God rather than on their particular circumstances.

Each situation, no matter how closely it resembles another, must be examined individually. There are no blanket exceptions to the Biblical ideal that the Lord be allowed to build the house, to populate the quiver. Any exception must be carefully tried and justified beyond a shadow of a doubt. It must truly be an *exception*, which means that it would apply only to a very small minority of believers. And such justification requires an obvious moral obligation and the express leading of God unto His glory. While a couple may have a legitimate reason to deviate from the Biblical ideal, before accepting that motive it "must be subjected to the scrutiny of faith and a good conscience in the light of revealed truth."[11]

Couples also should take the test of sincerity before deciding to limit their family. This test has only one question: Do you see the possibility of limiting conception as a sacrifice or as a relief?[12] In view of the strong Biblical perspective that children are God's gifts and blessings, an honest answer reveals much about the couples' true desire and motive.

A prayerful, honest examination of any motive is crucial for couples seeking to determine if they should practice contraception. If they feel compelled to abandon the Biblical ideal, they must supply the burden of proof for their action. They must ensure they are being directed by and for God, not by and for their own interests.

If they decide to limit conception, they must be sure they do so with a Biblical perspective and godly attitude. Under no circumstances should such a decision be an attempt to take God's place as the Creator and ruler of the world. Nor should a couple dare to challenge the basic structures of God's creation order or His command to "Be fruitful and multiply" (Genesis 1:28). While God has given men and women responsibilities on this earth, we must remember He is still Lord and King.

Christians also must remember that while the Fall opened the door to exceptions to the Biblical ideal, it did not make the exceptions the rule. The ideal—not the exceptions—should remain the goal of all believers. They should desire for God to build their family. The number and timing of their children should remain in His hands, unless He clearly has guided them to practice contraception. And since children are a blessing, any decision to prevent their birth must be made with a sense of disappointment, not relief.

That is not to say children bring no difficulties.

Certainly they present a challenge. But rather than seeking to avoid that challenge, we are to meet it in faith.

> By making what we think is a judicious intervention in the course of nature are we not allowing a calculating need for security to take precedence over confidence and faith in God? The bringing forth of children is *always* an incalculable venture; the bearing of a child is not without danger nor is its rearing without an element of risk. . . . From these "possibilities" there can come anxiety, which either becomes the material of faith (Ps. 73:23-28) or tempts us to meet it with the calculating prudence of security. The danger of this second reaction is that it may . . . turn out to be not only faithlessness . . . but may actually represent itself as being an act of responsible faith and thus put on the mask as an "angel of light" (II Cor. 11:14). Then what is represented to be a responsible act of omission . . . is in actuality only an untrusting anxiety which results in an excess of blind need for security.
>
> It is very often difficult to draw the line between security grounded upon the responsibility of faith . . . and

the need for security that grows out of unbelief. Birth control confronts us especially urgently with the question of *self*-control, because the dangers and uncertainties (the symptoms of "being-in-the-world") are cause for constant anxiety and therefore furnish an inexhaustible stock of reasons which appear to give us the right not to allow new life to come into being. The ability we have to act upon these reasons at any time and without incurring any risk by the use of technical means increases our readiness to claim them.

Therefore, faith will prove itself again and again, as Karl Barth so finely says, in "the conscious and resolute refusal . . . of the possibility of refusing, i.e., the joyful willingness to have children and therefore to become parents."[13]

Faith clearly will prove itself in the lives of individuals. By trusting God and following His plan, husbands and wives will experience the abundant life He intends. They will be walking in faith and thus growing in their trust in our faithful and loving God. They will know the joy of obedience and, Lord willing, the joy of helping create and nurture life.

The implications of following the Biblical ideal also could reach far beyond the individuals. Families, the church, and our society at large could benefit. We now will consider some of these implications of believers living according to these convictions.

Two Related Issues

We have argued that the Biblical ideal is that family planning should be God's planning. When this prerogative is arrogated by the couple to itself, whether by spacing children or limiting family size, they are making a cutoff point on how many blessings a family is willing to accept. In light of the data, two questions would have to be faced:[14] Does not limiting as a family planning method *separate* sex from reproduction? Is not spacing an attempt to usurp God's providence by self-crafting one's family?

We have also, however, stated that because of the Fall contraception may be a *necessary* exception to the ideal in some limited instances. If this is the case, two other issues arise which must at least be mentioned.

First, what about a childless marriage? In other words, in light of the Biblical ideal, is it proper for a couple to choose to have no children? Most who have addressed this subject agree that if the decision to remain childless is based on the desire to not have children, this decision is wrong. For example,

> . . . in view of the fact that children are
> a divine blessing promised to the cou-

> ple any sexual union in which children
> are not wanted cannot be considered a
> genuine marriage, notwithstanding its
> ecclesiastical consecration.[15]

> ... a marriage in which the desire for a
> child is consistently excluded ... is in
> contradiction to the meaning of mar-
> riage itself and to the blessing which
> God has bestowed upon marriage
> through the birth of a child.[16]

> The deliberate and permanent desire
> to ward off the coming of children
> must be condemned as fundamentally
> selfish and sinful.[17]

May there be cases where a couple, for what they feel are compelling, God-honoring reasons, must remain childless? Possibly. But this condition is surely a rare exception and must be one not of desire, but of sacrifice. It would appear that generally speaking to agree to avoid children is to agree not to marry.

The second issue is closely tied in with the first: What about permanent contraception? In other words, in light of our conclusions about the Biblical ideal, is permanent contraception (i.e., a vasectomy or tubal ligation) ever legitimate? Perhaps, under *highly* unusual circumstances, a couple would be compelled to have one partner sterilized. Such reasons are few, however, and must not be accepted lightly (indeed, we would give strong cautions against it, for this is a *major* decision and often has grave unforeseen consequences[18]). Generally, the question of limiting conception is a one-at-a-time decision. Couples should seek God's will for that particular time and circumstance, not for the whole future. Permanent contraception should be considered only as a last resort and must be mandated by the situation and God's express leading. The general rule must be that

> . . . contraception designed to prevent
> conception through the whole course
> of a marriage would go contrary to the
> intent of the Creator as revealed in His
> blessing to the first couple (Gen 1:28).[19]

In choosing such a course of action, couples must justify not only their prevention of the creation of life, but also their intentional destruction of a healthy bodily function. They must acknowledge God as the Creator of their own bodies as well as the Creator of their offspring. Is it clearly His will they they tamper with His creation in that way? Again, an extreme moral obligation may cause them to answer, "Yes," but the burden of proof lies with that couple. And as with all decisions to limit conception, this one must be viewed as a sacrifice, not as a relief.

PART 4

WHAT DOES IT ALL MEAN?

CHAPTER 10

THE TRUTH AND ITS CONSEQUENCES

No man (or woman) is an island. Adam and Eve learned that after they bit into the forbidden fruit. They probably never had dreamed anyone else would be affected by that one act. As we well know, billions of people have been.

Similarly, our actions affect others. If we run a stop sign, another driver might need to screech his brakes and find a constructive outlet for his anger. When we barbecue steaks in our backyard, our neighbors salivate. If we let an obviously hassled shopper go before us in the grocery line, her frown may turn into a smile. As we walk in the power of the Holy Spirit, others see the radiant light of Christ and are drawn to Him.

What then are the ramifications of following the Biblical ideal for contraception? When husbands and wives obey God's will by leaving conception under His control, whose lives are touched, and how? We will now look at some likely implications.

Strengthening the Family

If Christians followed the Biblical ideal, the foundational and most immediate result would be seen in the home. Families would be strengthened, primarily because unless unusual circumstances mandated that the mother work outside the home, she would be there to function in her God-given role.

The wife in the household is the "heart," the "inside center" of the family. She directs a set of family activities essential to the functioning of the family. The husband is the "head." He both directs a set of family functions and is over the wife's activities, but he cannot "keep the body alive" without her.[1]

Certainly, to have the mother home the family must pay a price. Especially for those couples long-accustomed to two salaries, reverting to a single income may seem a great sacrifice. Yet, is it not for a much greater cause? Couples must pay the price, and should do so willingly, to restore family strength. Achieving family good, rather than acquiring material goods, should be the priority.

In addition to strengthening the family unit, following the Biblical ideal will strengthen its members. Husbands and wives will grow in ways possible only through the discipline and self-sacrifice of rearing children. Their faith will increase as they are compelled to trust the Lord for wisdom and for their children's provision and safety. Regarding their offspring as a sacred trust, of whose care they must render an account, parents will frequently consult God concerning them. Thus, their walk with Him will grow stronger.

Joy also will abound in the home where God is Lord of the womb and children are received as a gift from Him. Families will experience the loving and sharing unity God intends. And that joy and unity will not leave when the children do. Adult offspring who honor their parents bring them much satisfaction, and "grandchildren are the crown of old men" (Proverbs 17:6). Parents will avoid the loneliness of old age by embracing the love of their children and grandchildren.

In addition to receiving love, parents also should receive their children's support. "Like arrows in the hand of a warrior" (Psalm 127:4), their children should provide protection and security. God does not intend for the elderly to base their security on bank accounts, life insurance, and nursing homes. Instead, grown children are to care for their aging parents' needs, just as their parents provided for them in earlier years. As Paul taught, "[I]f any widow has children or grandchildren, let them first learn to practice piety in regard to their own family, and to make some return to their parents; for this is acceptable in the sight of God" (1 Timothy 5:4).

The prevalent control mentality has barred many from the joy and support of a strong family. Some miss out because they think they control conception, but when they eventually want children, they find they no longer can conceive them. Others ardently desire children, but they are infertile, and the babies they might have adopted have been aborted. Some refuse to make the temporary sacrifices a family requires, and thus refuse the lifelong—and eternal—rewards.

If Christians follow the Biblical ideal regarding contraception, however, they will experience the benefits of strong, loving, supportive families. And their control-mentality neighbors will notice. The example of these Christian families will show the world that God's plan brings joy to men and women, as well as glory to Him.

Strengthening the Body of Christ

Adopting a Biblical attitude toward the family also will have vital and long-range implications for the church. It not only will benefit its individual members, but will strengthen the corporate body as a whole and enhance its witness to the world. Let's look at two primary ways this will occur.

First, Scripture indicates the home is a training-ground for ministry in the church. Paul taught that anyone aspiring to leadership in the church family must first prove he can rule his own family. "He must be one who manages his own household well, keeping his children under control with all dignity (but if a man does not know how to manage his own household, how will he take care of the church of God?)" (1 Timothy 3:4, 5).

In these verses Paul links managing the household with caring for the church; he uses the terms almost synonymously. One cannot Biblically manage or rule his children without caring for them. He cannot rule with a control mentality or for selfish interests. Nor can he cling to his "right" to a carefree life and thus reject his God-given responsibility to bear and rear children. He must accept the gifts God gives him and responsibly care for them.

A husband who sacrificially manages his household so he can care for its members becomes better qualified to manage the church and care for its members. His training at home prepares him to welcome and patiently nurture spiritual babies and to discipline older believers when necessary. He is willing and better equipped to help meet the needs of God's children in all stages of their growth. Thus, the husband, his family, and the church are strengthened by his obedience to God's mandates.

Second, a Biblical attitude toward the family can lead to a fuller release and better channeling of gifts and energy in the church. Instead of a few people doing most of the work, as is too often the case, the majority will share the load. Members will have learned to sacrifice for and work together in their families. Consequently they will exhibit the same attitude and behavior in the church. Their interdependence, mutual self-giving, and loving service will carry over into God's family.

As a result, the church will be seen as caring for those in need. Consider the communal attitude evident in the early church, whose members sold their possessions so they could give to others (Acts 2:44, 45). As described in Acts 4:34, 35, no one will remain needy because believers will share liberally. Sacrificial giving will replace the selfish individualistic living rampant in the church today.

This concern and the church's overall attitude toward life and the family will be a powerful witness to the world. Rather than seeing the church as an organization that seeks its own comfort, society will see it as an organism that seeks to help create and nurture life. In a world that tries to prevent the intrusion of life, the church will warmly welcome it. The contrast will speak loudly.

And the contrast will be evident in the homes of individual members, which is where most people encounter the church. "If we welcome life, regardless of family size, we shall treasure it above appearances—including the appearance of the kitchen floor under the impact of many feet. If you know the price of that, do not imagine that your neighbor isn't aware of it, too. And your neighbor's children."[2]

By fulfilling God's creative purposes, Christian families will offer a striking testimony to the world. Nonbelievers will clearly see God has a plan for the family, and that their own attitudes and actions fall outside of it. Thus, the families in the church, by following God's design, will serve as a judgment, as well as a promise and a hope, for the world.

Strengthening Society

Couples who try to control life through contraception and abortion generally achieve their desired end: few, if any, children are born to them. But that is not all they are achieving. They are dramatically reducing the number of children born in our country, which has grave implications for our society as a whole. French demographer Pierre Chaunu calls this concerted effort to limit conception "the strangest collective suicide of history."[3]

As a result of this decline in birthrate, our society will have a high proportion of elderly, with a low number of young workers. Who will make the Social Security payments on which the elderly depend? And who in our self-centered society will meet their other needs? The role of the elderly will be an increasing concern. And unemployment will continue to haunt us, since fewer schoolteachers and others whose jobs depend on children will be needed.[4]

Again, the Biblical ideal offers hope. Christians can restore health to our society by obeying the command to "Be fruitful and multiply" (Genesis 1:28). As those who trust in God, they can confidently reproduce even as others despair. And, as stated before, they will care lovingly for the elderly. These Christian families will be godly examples, and their strength will bring strength to their communities.

Following the Biblical ideal will clearly benefit the family, the church, and our society as a whole. It will offer stability and restore order to God's creation as people submit to His design. It also will affect society's stance on abortion, euthanasia, and other issues relating to the control of life.

The Domino Effect

Do you remember, as a child, strategically lining up many dominoes on end? Then, perhaps after calling an audience, you gently pushed the first domino. To your delight, it knocked down the next, which knocked down the next, and soon all had toppled.

Our attitude toward contraception is much like that initial domino. If we insist on taking control of life by preventing or limiting conception, it will dramatically affect our family, our church, and our entire society. They will continue to weaken, and our witness to the world will lack power.

Submitting to the Biblical ideal regarding contraception also has far-reaching implications. If we allow God to be Lord of the womb, we will strengthen our Christian walk, our family, our church, our society, and our witness. Rather than fighting against God's plan, we will help fulfill it. We will glorify the one who alone merits glory, and we will experience His abundant blessings. Then we joyfully will echo the words of the psalmist:

> Behold, children are a gift
> of the LORD;
> the fruit of the womb is a reward.
> Like arrows in the hand of a warrior,
> So are the children of one's youth.
> How blessed is the man whose quiver
> is full of them.
>
> (Psalm 127:3-5)

CHAPTER 11

THE RIGHT QUESTION ANSWERED

Still thinking about their Biblical examination of con-
traception and their conclusions, Sue turns to Carl.
"You know, I'm thankful we chose to study and follow
God's teaching rather than follow the crowd."

"Me, too," Carl nods. "It would have been easy to
adopt the world's mentality, but God has called us to have
the mind of Christ—not the mind of our society."

"He also has called us to live according to His will,
not our desires. But how quickly I lose sight of that! After
all, the world tells me to look out for myself and my interests. It says I should be self-centered, not God-centered."

"I think we all need to be reminded continually that
God is Lord, and that we are to live for Him," Carl says. "I
guess that's why it's so important to spend time each day
in His Word and in prayer."

"Yes, daily—in fact, moment by moment—we need
to acknowledge Him as Lord in every area of our lives."

"Including the area of our family. His Word teaches
that a primary purpose of our marriage is to have chil-

dren. We are commanded to multiply, and we need to joyfully submit to that."

"There's always a chance He will not give us children, but we need to leave that in His hands," Sue adds. "We need to live by faith, trusting our sovereign, wise, loving God to give us children if and when He chooses."

"If He does bless us with children, we need to gladly receive them as gifts—no matter how many He gives us and no matter when."

"And I need to gladly fulfill my role as wife and mother. I need to see my responsibility as God designed it—not as the world has maligned it."

"How important it is that we keep God's perspective in everything. He is the sovereign giver of life. That is His domain—not ours."

"And, while He uses children to discipline us, He also uses them to bring us much joy."

"Joy that will last our lifetime—joy and love from our children, their children . . . and maybe even their children." Carl smiles.

"When we are old, it will be good to know we have a family to love us and help care for us if necessary."

"And while we're young, it is good to know that we can trust God to supply what we need to provide for any children He gives us."

"Yes, He'll supply the necessary spiritual, emotional, and material resources."

"I used to think we should practice contraception so we could provide better for our children. I thought we should wait to start a family until I earned more money.

Now I realize I just didn't want to make financial sacrifices. We might have to do without a few things we want, but we certainly could afford a child even if God gave us one right away."

"I remember us talking about limiting our family size so we wouldn't contribute to the overpopulation problem, but now I see that the whole idea of 'population explosion' really is a myth," Sue says. "Nor do we need to ensure a long enough adjustment period before we start a family. God will give us whatever time we need."

"As we considered the potential motives for practicing contraception, I realized we really have no legitimate reason," Carl says. "Any departure from the Biblical ideal would be for our comfort and convenience, not for God's glory."

"Before, I would have used a number of those reasons to rationalize controlling the timing and number of our children. Until I measured them against Scripture and took them to God in prayer, they sounded pretty good. Now they sound self-centered, not God-centered."

"Even motives that sound good may not be God's will," Carl says. "For example, can you imagine if Moses' mother and father had taken the 'reasonable' approach and practiced contraception, so they would not risk giving birth to a son who would be put to death?"

"Who would have led the Israelites out of captivity?"

"Or what if David's parents were concerned about providing for their family, so they limited it to seven sons?"

"I sure would miss all his psalms. Who would have been king . . . or carried on the messianic line?"

Carl shrugged. "People may try to come up with convincing arguments for trying to control conception, but it clearly is best to leave that up to God."

"It's hard to imagine situations where Christians should practice contraception," Sue says.

"Because of the Fall some couples may have valid reasons to control conception. Before determining that, however, they need to evaluate their circumstances carefully and prayerfully. They must sincerely seek God's will."

"The burden of proof obviously lies with anyone considering restricting the size of their family," Sue adds. "And any such decision must be considered a sacrifice, not a relief."

"Also, a reason to practice contraception must be viewed as an exception, not the rule. I see now that God's intent for most couples is to not make any effort to control if and when they have children."

"Yes, as we've seen over and over again, we'll be blessed in many ways as we follow the Biblical ideal and obey God."

"We'll experience great joy, we'll be conformed to the image of Christ, and our faith will increase."

"Our family also will be stronger," Sue adds.

"Which will help strengthen our church, and even our society and its morals."

"We also will be a witness to our neighbors. Our attitude will be such a sharp contrast to the world's that they certainly will take note."

"Yes, whenever we obey God and submit to His

plan, we help reveal Him to the world. And isn't that our goal?"

"I once thought having children might hinder our ministry, but now I see that it will enhance it."

"By fulfilling one of God's purposes for us—bearing and raising children—we will help fulfill His other purposes, including evangelism."

"Only God could design a scheme that works together so well to accomplish His purposes. We tend to think we know how we should glorify Him, but He is the one who truly knows best."

Carl thinks for a moment. "That is why He is Lord."

"And that's why He should be Lord of the womb."

NOTES

CHAPTER TWO: *The Development of a Contraceptive Attitude*

1. Louis H. Gray, "Children (Iranian)," in ed. James Hastings, *Encyclopedia of Religion and Ethics*, Volume 3 (Edinburgh: T & T Clark, 1931), p. 544.
2. Norman E. Himes, *Medical History of Contraception* (New York: Schocken Books, 1970), p. 105.
3. E. Anwyl, "Children (Celtic)," in ed. Hastings, *Encyclopedia of Religion*, p. 529.
4. John T. Noonan, Jr., *Contraception: A History of Its Treatment by the Catholic Theologians and Canonists* (New York: The American Library, 1967), pp. 23, 24.
5. M. J. Huth, "Birth Control Movement," in *New Catholic Encyclopedia*, Volume 2 (New York: McGraw-Hill, 1967), p. 576.
6. Noonan, *Contraception*, pp. 468, 469.
7. Jeremy Jackson, "The Shadow of Death," in ed. Richard Ganz, *Thou Shalt Not Kill* (New Rochelle, NY: Arlington House, 1978), pp. 77-91.
8. Jeremy Jackson, "Seed Time and Harvest: The Building of the Lord's House," *Life and Light* (Summer/Fall 1985): 4.
9. Huth, "Birth Control Movement," *New Catholic Encyclopedia*, p. 576.
10. Noonan, *Contraception*, pp. 484-486.
11. George Gilder, *Sexual Suicide* (New York: Quadrangle, 1973), p. 252.
12. Christopher Lasch, *The Culture of Narcissism* (New York: W. W. Norton, 1979), p. xvi.
13. Daniel Yankelovich, "New Rules: Searching for Self-Fulfillment in a World Turned Upside Down," *Psychology Today* 15 (April 1981): 36.
14. Germaine Greer, *Sex and Destiny: The Politics of Human Fertility* (New York: Harper and Row, 1984), p. 2.
15. *Encyclopedia Britannica*, 15th edition, s.v. "Birth Control."
16. A. M. Nicholi, "Moral Maturity," *Pastoral Renewal* 10 (July/August 1985): 1.

17. See Jon Johnston, *Will Evangelicalism Survive Its Own Popularity?* (Grand Rapids, MI: Zondervan, 1980).
18. Jackson, "Seedtime and Harvest," p. 4.
19. R. M. Fagley, *The Population Explosion and Christian Responsibility* (New York: Oxford University Press, 1960), p. 192.
20. J. J. Farraher, "Contraception," in *New Catholic Encyclopedia* (New York: McGraw-Hill, 1974), p. 103.
21. *Ibid.*
22. As Noonan notes (*Contraception*, p. 581), it was beginning with the Anglican decision in 1929/1930 that a large number of denominations publicly abandoned the absolute prohibition of contraception by married couples (see *ibid.* for a listing). One of the few which did not abandon their original prohibition was the Greek Orthodox Church, which continued to condemn the "unnatural evil" of "escape from begetting children and nurturing them" (*ibid.*, p. 582).
23. "With the new spirit of freedom in almost every area of man's experience came the changing standards in the specific area of the prohibition of contraceptives with many Christian groups" (Lloyd A. Kalland, "Views and Positions of the Christian Church—An Historical Review," in *Birth Control and the Christian*, eds. W. Spitzer and C. Saylor [Wheaton, IL: Tyndale, 1969], p. 446). It is also interesting to note that this change in viewpoint took place right in the middle of the modernist-fundamentalist controversy. This was at the time when Enlightenment thinking took over leadership in many of the mainline denominations.
24. J. Grundel, "Birth Control," in ed. Bernard Stoeckle, *The Concise Dictionary of Christian Ethics* (New York: Seabury, 1979), p. 25.
25. M. O. Vincent, "A Christian View of Contraception," *Christianity Today* 13 (November 8, 1968): 14.
26. Dwight H. Small, *Design for Christian Marriage* (Old Tappan, NJ: Revell, 1971), p. 112.

CHAPTER THREE: *Marriage, Sex, and the Pursuit of Happiness*

1. Ronald S. Wallace, *Calvin's Doctrine of the Christian Life* (Tyler TX: Geneva Divinity School Press, 1959), p. 161.
2. See H. C. Leupold, *Exposition of Genesis*, Volume 1 (Grand Rapids, MI: Baker, 1950), p. 96; and Mary Pride, *The Way Home* (Westchester, IL: Crossway Books, 1985), p. 20.
3. See Stephen Clark, *Man and Woman in Christ* (Ann Arbor, MI: Servant, 1980), pp. 20-22.
4. Pride, *The Way Home*, p. 20.
5. See P. E. Hughes, *Christian Ethics in Secular Society* (Grand Rapids, MI: Baker, 1983), p. 151.

6. *Ibid.*, p. 167.
7. R. M. Fagley, *The Population Explosion and Christian Responsibility* (New York: Oxford University Press, 1960), p. 221.
8. Norman Geisler, *Ethics: Alternatives and Issues* (Grand Rapids, MI: Zondervan, 1971), p. 216.
9. C. Everett Koop, "Contraception," in ed. Carl F. H. Henry, *Dictionary of Christian Ethics* (Grand Rapids, MI: Baker, 1973), p. 138.
10. Bruce Waltke, "The Old Testament and Birth Control," *Christianity Today* 13 (November 8, 1968): 6.
11. Geisler makes this and the previous argument in *Ethics*, pp. 213, 214.
12. See M. O. Vincent, "A Christian View of Contraception," *Christianity Today* 13 (November 8, 1968): 14. Also, C. E. Cerling, "Abortion and Contraception in Scripture," *Christian Scholars Review* 2 (1971): 57, 58.
13. Derek Kidner, *Genesis* (Downers Grove, IL: InterVarsity Press, 1967), p. 52.
14. Otto A. Piper, *The Biblical View of Sex and Marriage* (New York: Charles Scribner's Sons, 1960), p. 32.

CHAPTER FOUR: *The Place of Children and Women*

1. This last argument is made in Letha and John Scanzoni, *Men, Women, and Change* (New York: McGraw-Hill, 1976), p. 377.
2. Derek Kidner, *Psalms*, Volume 2 (Downers Grove, IL: InterVarsity Press, 1973), p. 442.
3. It is obvious from the contexts that these examples are all in a sense "exceptional" cases. However, it must be affirmed at the same time that they still speak the truth about God's unique role in conception.
4. Jeremy Jackson, "The Shadow of Death," in ed. Richard Ganz, *Thou Shalt Not Kill* (New Rochelle, NY: Arlington House, 1978), p. 109, n. 58.
5. Kenneth Gangel, "Toward a Biblical Theology of Marriage and Family, Part One: Pentateuch and Historical Books," *Journal of Psychology and Theology* 5 (Winter 1977): 57.
6. R. E. O. White, *A Christian Handbook to the Psalms* (Grand Rapids, MI: Eerdmans, 1984), p. 190.
7. It is proper to note that God's sovereignty over the womb is similar to His sovereignty in other areas—it also involves man's responsibility. God has established natural processes. He generally leaves the process in place and expects us to act responsibly. Of course, He can and does intervene if and when He desires. Most pregnancies are the result of a natural, God-ordained pro-

cess. We are responsible to honor His commands/desires as we are involved in that process. Yet, at the same time God is sovereignly in control of all that goes on. As in other areas where the sovereignty of God and the responsibility of man are seen (e.g., in our salvation), this will have to ultimately remain inscrutable to our finite minds. But we must not allow this inscrutability to fog our minds into thinking that God's commands are not to be obeyed, that we may set up ourselves as the ones in control of the arena of conception and life.

Perhaps the theological doctrine of "providence" is a better term than sovereignty in this case, although it must be properly defined so as to retain its full implications, which implications do indeed contain the idea of the sovereign control of God. "An adequate definition of God requires his overlordship of the history of all that is" (N. M. de S. Cameron, "Providence," in *New Dictionary of Theology*, eds. Ferguson and Wright [Downers Grove, IL: InterVarsity Press, 1988], p. 541). Providence may be seen as "the beneficent outworking of God's sovereignty whereby all events are directed and disposed to bring about those purposes of glory and good for which the universe was made. These events include the actions of free agents, which while remaining free, personal and responsible are also the intended actions of those agents. Providence thus encompasses both natural and personal events, setting them alike within the purposes of God" (*ibid.*).

8. Mary Pride, *The Way Home* (Westchester, IL: Crossway Books, 1985), p. 41. Whether or not all children are always a blessing is a question that arises (e.g., children born out of wedlock, from adultery, from rape, etc.). In dealing with this question, however, it must be noted that we have imported other factors (*sin!*) into the equation which add complexity to the issue at hand and make the answering of the question very difficult and beyond the scope of this book. We are speaking to Christians, to those who are under the Lordship of Jesus Christ and the authority of His Word. For them, Scripture is clear that children are indeed a blessing and are to be received that way.

9. P. E. Hughes, *Christian Ethics in Secular Society* (Grand Rapids, MI: Baker, 1983), p. 167.

10. Stephen Clark, *Man and Woman in Christ* (Ann Arbor, MI: Servant, 1980), p. 23.

11. Pride, *The Way Home*, pp. 41, 42.

12. T. W. Wallbank, A. M. Taylor, and N. M. Bailkey, *Civilization Past and Present*, 7th edition (Glenview, IL: Scott, Foresman and Co., 1976), p. 161.

13. R. N. Whybray, *The Book of Proverbs*, The Cambridge Bible Commentary (Cambridge, Great Britain: Cambridge University Press, 1972), p. 184.
14. Susan Foh, *Women and the Word of God* (Phillipsburg, NJ: Presbyterian and Reformed, 1979), pp. 227-230.

CHAPTER FIVE: *God's Perspective on Life*

1. For much of the thinking in this chapter, I am indebted to Jeremy Jackson, "Seedtime and Harvest: The Building of the Lord's House," *Life and Light* (Summer/Fall 1985): 4-6.
2. *Ibid.*, p. 5.
3. O. Michel, "Faith," in ed. Colin Brown, *New International Dictionary of New Testament Theology*, Volume 1 (Grand Rapids, MI: Zondervan, 1975), p. 600.

CHAPTER SIX: *The Biblical Ideal for Contraception*

1. Methods have not been addressed in this book because they are not the issue. The issue is whether or not contraception is valid. Of course, an affirmative answer would lead to the question of methods, but we have not arrived at such an answer.

    Many who have questioned only methods, however, have concluded that artificial contraception is wrong, but "natural" contraception is permissible. Yet, the issue is not that of choosing the "right" method of contraception. The use of *any* method is an attempt to avoid conception, an attempt to avoid the God-given responsibility of bearing children. It is a refusal to follow God's design and to fulfill a primary purpose of marriage. It is an effort to control the womb rather than to trust God.

    It also should be remembered that in 1 Corinthians 7, Paul admonishes married couples to not abstain from intercourse except for the purpose of prayer. And in the Old Testament, couples were to abstain only during the wife's menstruation, a practice that actually would tend to *increase* fertility.
2. A. W. Tozer, *The Knowledge of the Holy* (New York: Harper and Row, 1961), p. 70.

CHAPTER SEVEN: *Are There Exceptions?*

1. John Murray, *Principles of Conduct* (Grand Rapids, MI: Eerdmans, 1957), p. 44.
2. Helmut Thielicke, *The Ethics of Sex*, trans. John W. Doberstein (New York: Harper and Row, 1964), p. 203.

3. Michael C. Jaskilka, "A Biblical Perspective of Genetic Manipulation" (Th.M. thesis, Western Conservative Baptist Seminary, 1976), p. 52.
4. Francis A. Schaeffer, *Pollution and the Death of Man* (Wheaton, IL: Tyndale House, 1970), p. 69.
5. Richard Fagley, *The Population Explosion and Christian Responsibility* (New York: Oxford University Press, 1960), p. 208.
6. Thielicke, *Ethics of Sex*, pp. 210, 211.
7. *Ibid.*, p. 204. Thielicke adds:

> If, for example, our willingness to exercise this consideration should lead to the conclusion that contraception is permissible, this will certainly not be because we argue that "such is life" (*c'est la vie*), but rather because we know that in this situation—we are purposely phrasing this guardedly—the begetting of children is fulfilling only *one* side of the created [*schopfungsmassige*] relationship of marriage and that this introduces a *conflict* in the order of creation which it did not have "from the beginning" (Matt. 19:8). Here something is being "put asunder" which God has "joined together." By expressing it in this way we respect the claim of the order of creation and allow it to continue to be a dam against the inevitable degeneration that must result as soon as the alleged realities are made the standard of judgment instead of being themselves subjected to judgment.

8. Jeremy Jackson, "The Shadow of Death," in ed. Richard Ganz, *Thou Shalt Not Kill* (New Rochelle, NY: Arlington House, 1978), p. 93. Others who have reached the same conclusion—i.e., that the burden of proof rests with those who would restrict the size of their family—include: John W. Montgomery, "How to Decide the Birth Control Issue," *Christianity Today* (March 4, 1966): 582; Bruce Waltke, "The Old Testament and Birth Control," *Christianity Today* (November 8, 1968): 6; and John Jefferson Davis, *Evangelical Ethics* (Phillipsburg, NJ: Presbyterian and Reformed, 1985), pp. 48, 49.

> Davis marshals impressive evidence *against* contraception from church history, Scripture, and the logical implications of Scripture. Note the following summary from a review of Davis's book by Jeff Guimont in *Trinity Journal* 8 NS, 2 (Fall 1987): 248-250 (page numbers are from *Evangelical Ethics*):

> Some of the OT evidence cited can be summarized quickly as: (1) the "mandate" (p. 45) to Adam and Eve to "... be fruitful, multiply and fill the earth" (Gen 1:28); (2) the repetition of this command to Noah and his sons (Gen 9:1); (3) the "promise of

fruitfulness in procreation is an important feature of the Abrahamic covenant, repeated on a number of different occasions" (Gen 12:2, 13:16, 15:5, 17:6, 18:18, 22:7, 8, 26:4, 24, 28:14, 35:11) (p. 46); (4) the judgment of God upon Onan for refusing his levirate duty (Gen 39:9, 10); (5) the apodictic proscription (Lev 18:19) of menstrual intercourse which, as Davis rightly cites, would be "anti-contraceptive [in] effect" (p. 46); (6) the exclusion from the covenant community of those who were emasculated (Deut 23:1); (7) the Psalmists' expression of the blessed state of those with children (Ps 127:3, 128:3); and (8) the desire of YHWH for godly offspring (Mal 2:15). Davis concludes, ". . . the Old Testament expresses a clearly pro-natalist philosophy . . . it would not seem easy to justify contraception on the basis of the Old Testament outlook" (p. 46).

As Davis advances to NT teaching and implications on the subject, he is forced even further toward a "pro-natalist outlook."

It is interesting, however, as Guimont notes, that Davis is not willing to allow the evidence to speak. He seeks to permit contraception even in the face of all the Biblical evidence he has gathered against it. We agree with Guimont that this is a case of allowing "one's presuppositions [to] control one's conclusions" (p. 250) and "Little more than an avoidance of the conclusion demanded by the data" (p. 249).

9. Obviously wisdom is necessary, a Biblical wisdom which is derived from the fear of the Lord (Proverbs 9:10; 1:7). Stott's four epochs, corresponding to the four realities we have already discussed, may be useful in providing a framework for making God-honoring decisions (*Involvement, Volume I: Being a Responsible Christian in a Non-Christian Society* [Old Tappan, NJ: Revell, 1984], p. 61. See the extended discussion on pp. 53-72):

. . . first the Creation ("the good"), secondly the Fall ("the evil"), thirdly the Redemption ("the new"), and fourthly the Consummation ("the perfect"). This four-fold biblical reality enables Christians to survey the historical landscape within its proper horizons. It supplies the perspective from which to view the unfolding process between two eternities, the vision of God working out His purpose. It gives us a framework in which to fit everything, a way of integrating our understanding, the possibility of thinking straight, even about the most complex issues. . . . For the four events or epochs . . . especially when grasped in relation to one another, teach major truths about

God, man, and society which give direction to our Christian thinking.

CHAPTER EIGHT: *Social Motives for Contraception*

1. Robert P. Meye, "New Testament Texts Bearing on the Problem of the Control of Human Reproduction," in *Birth Control and the Christian*, eds. Spitzer and Saylor (Wheaton, IL: Tyndale, 1969), pp. 36, 37.
2. Such reasons are cited in John Noonan, *Contraception: A History of Its Treatment by the Catholic Theologians and Canonists* (New York: The American Library, 1967), pp. 198, 199, 270; R. M. Fagley, *The Population Explosion and Christian Responsibility* (New York: Oxford University Press, 1960), p. 208; and Helmut Thielicke, *The Ethics of Sex*, trans. John W. Doberstein (New York: Harper and Row, 1964), p. 200.
3. Thielicke, *Ethics of Sex*, p. 201.
4. For example, see Fagley, *Population Explosion*, pp. 33-39; George Forrell and W. Lazareth, *Population Perils* (Philadelphia: Fortress Press, 1979); Paul Ehrlich, *The Population Bomb* (New York: Ballantine Books, 1968).
5. J. R. Kasun, "The Population Bomb Threat: A Look at the Facts," *Intellect* (June 1977), quoted in James Weber, *Grow or Die!* (New Rochelle, NY: Arlington House, 1977), pp. 412-414.
6. "Roots of the Hunger Problem," *World Christian* 4 (November-December 1985): 33, 34.
7. As quoted in Max Heine, "Population Controllers Are Saying: 'Be Fruitless and Subtract,'" *World* (September 23, 1989): 11.
8. Cited in The Hunger Project's *Ending Hunger: An Idea Whose Time Has Come* (New York: Praeger, 1985), pp. 45, 46, 173.
9. Jean Mayer, "Food and Population: The Wrong Problem?," *Daedalus* (Summer 1964): 835ff.
10. See the article by Yedek and Robbins, "Once Again, Disaster in Ethiopia," in the *Chicago Tribune* (January 14, 1988), Section 1: 27. They note the theft and exploitation carried on by the government in relation to the aid sent, as well as the destructive political policies (such as having an estimated 75 percent of the national budget going to the military, leaving a pittance for developing agriculture—the main defense against famine).
11. Heine, "Population Controllers . . .," p. 11.
12. John R. W. Stott, *Involvement Volume I: Being a Responsible Christian in a Non-Christian Society* (Old Tappan, NJ: Revell, 1984), pp. 165, 166.

13. *Ibid.*, p. 165.
14. See, for example, Marvin Olasky, ed., *Freedom, Justice, and Hope* (Westchester, IL: Crossway Books, 1988); Ronald Nash, *Poverty and Wealth* (Westchester, IL: Crossway Books, 1988).
15. Available from the Villars Committee on Relief and Development, Office of Communications, P.O. Box 26010, Philadelphia, PA 19128.
16. See, e.g., P. T. Bauer, *Equality, the Third World, and Economic Delusion* (Cambridge, MA: Harvard University Press, 1981), p.49ff.
17. Cf. Heine, "Population Controllers . . .," p. 11.
18. Bauer, *Equality*, p. 51ff.
19. In his book *The Ultimate Resource* (Princeton, NJ: Princeton University Press, 1981), Julian Simon argues that ending hunger and poverty will occur as a result of larger, not smaller, populations, and as a result of more, not fewer, people. He posits that *people* are the "ultimate resource." As an example, in the book he comments on the following topics (pp. 5-8, with extended discussion in the remainder of the book):

Food. Contrary to popular impression, the per capita food situation has been improving for the three decades since WWII, the only decades for which we have acceptable data. We also know that famine has progressively diminished for at least the past century. And there is strong reason to believe that human nutrition will continue to improve into the indefinite future, even with continued population growth. [Additional people may be a benefit in the long run—p. 69, cf. Part II; population growth is likewise *not* the cause of too little food!—p. 80.]

Land. Agricultural land is not a fixed resource, as Malthus and many since Malthus have thought. Rather, the amount of agricultural land has been, and still is, increasing substantially, and it is likely to continue to increase where needed. . . .

Natural Resources. Hold your hat—our supplies of natural resources are not finite in any economic sense. Nor does past experience give reason to expect natural resources to become more scarce. Rather, if the past is any guide, natural resources will progressively become less scarce, and less costly, and will constitute a smaller proportion of our expenses in future years. And population growth is likely to have a long-run *beneficial* impact on the natural-resource situation.

Energy . . . the long-run future of our energy supply is at least as bright as that of other natural resources. . . . Finiteness is no problem here either. And the long-run impact of additional people is likely to speed the development of a cheap energy supply that is almost inexhaustible.

Pollution. This set of issues is as complicated as you wish to make it. But even many ecologists, as well as the bulk of economists, agree that population growth is not the villain in the creation and reduction of pollution. . . .

Pathological effects of population growth. This putative drawback of population growth is sheer myth. Its apparent source is faulty biological and psychological analogies with animal populations.

The standard of living. In the short run, additional children imply additional costs, though the costs to persons other than the children's parents are relatively small. In the longer run, however, per capita income is likely to be higher with a growing population than with a stationary one, both in more-developed and less-developed countries. Whether you . . . pay present costs for future benefits depends on how you weigh the future relative to the present; this is a value judgment.

Part II of Simon's book gives some of the positives of population growth while debunking some of the myths concerning supposed negatives. His conclusions are reinforced by Kasun in *The War Against Population.* Note also pages 42-45 in *Ending Hunger.*

20. Government-controlled measures to prevent conception, then, offer no solution at all. In fact, such measures would flagrantly violate God's purposes for a husband and wife. They "would seriously blur the fundamental structure of the order of creation . . . [and] make the exception the rule" (Thielicke, *Ethics of Sex,* pp. 218, 219).

21. Quoted in *Ending Hunger,* p. 91.

22. As Henry Morris comments:

Man has not yet filled the earth, in accordance with God's command; nevertheless, many people today are unduly alarmed over the so-called population explosion, urging government controls of various sorts to slow down population growth. . . . Even at the present level of man's technological knowledge, the earth could support a much larger population than it now holds. Obviously, it could not continue to grow indefinitely, without limit, but God no doubt has made adequate provision for such an eventuality.

The Genesis Record (Grand Rapids, MI: Baker, 1976), p. 76.

CHAPTER NINE: *Personal Motives for Contraception*

1. John Noonan, *Contraception: A History of Its Treatment by the Catholic Theologians and Canonists* (New York: The American Library, 1967), p. 71.
2. Quoted in Dwight Small, *Design for Christian Marriage* (Old Tappan, NJ: Revell, 1959), p. 118.
3. Germaine Greer, *Sex and Destiny: The Politics of Human Fertility* (New York: Harper and Row, 1984), pp. 185, 186.
4. Such arguments are found in V. Elving Anderson, "Genetics," in ed. Carl F. H. Henry, *Baker's Dictionary of Christian Ethics* (Grand Rapids, MI: Baker, 1973), p. 260; Paul Ramsey, *Fabricated Man* (New Haven, CT: Yale University Press, 1970), p. 57. See also Michael C. Jaskilka, "A Biblical Perspective of Genetic Manipulation" (Th.M. thesis, Western Conservative Baptist Seminary, 1976), pp. 67, 68.
5. Jack C. Willke and Barbara Willke, *Handbook on Abortion* (Cincinnati: Hayes, 1976), pp. 118, 119.
6. Philip E. Hughes, "Theological Principles in the Control of Human Life," in eds. Spitzer and Saylor, *Birth Control and the Christian* (Wheaton, IL: Tyndale, 1969), p. 148.
7. Adapted from contribution by John Galbreath, *Reader's Digest* (August 1982): 65.
8. Adam Clark, quoted in Charles H. Spurgeon, *The Treasury of David*, Volume 7, reprint (Grand Rapids, MI: Guardian Press, 1976), p. 38.
9. Rand Corporation, *Demographic Challenges in America's Future*, cited in Bill Baer and Kevin Perrotta, "Bearing Down: American Women's Declining Fertility—And Its Consequences," *Pastoral Renewal* 10 (September 1985): 24.
10. This fits in with the historical reasons for contraception cited by Noonan (*Contraception*): rationalistic thinking (p. 467), spiritual malaise (p. 464), and utilitarian ethics (p. 467). Modern man is simply carrying this same control mentality to new heights; cf. John Whitehead, *The End of Man* (Westchester, IL: Crossway Books, 1986).
11. Jeremy Jackson, "Seedtime and Harvest: The Building of the Lord's House," *Life and Light* (Summer/Fall 1985): 6.
12. *Ibid.*, p. 7.
13. Helmut Thielicke, *The Ethics of Sex*, trans. John W. Doberstein (New York: Harper and Row, 1964), pp. 220, 221.
14. Mary Pride, *The Way Home* (Westchester, IL: Crossway Books, 1985), pp. 76, 77.
15. Otto A. Piper, *The Biblical View of Sex and Marriage* (New York: Charles Scribner's Sons, 1960), p. 145.

16. Dietrich Bonhoeffer, *Ethics*, ed. Eberhard Bethage, trans. Neville H. Smith (New York: Macmillan, 1955), p. 176.
17. Roger Mehl, *Society and Love*, trans. James H. Farley (Philadelphia: Westminster, 1964), p. 196.
18. The personal testimony of Ann Kelly reveals one woman's experience with the gravity of such a decision. "Sterilization and an Unformed Conscience," *New Oxford Review* 52 (October 1985): 18-20. Mrs. Kelly recounts the story of undergoing sterilization after child number three because "I was feeling overwhelmed by babies, and I thought that if I became pregnant again I wouldn't be able to cope" (p. 18). Subsequently experiencing some trauma, she was led ultimately to a religious conversion. Afterwards, her reflections on sterilization included the following: ". . . the notions of God and man had gotten turned around. God is the Creator of all things, man being the crown of His creation. Man, as steward of creation, takes care of, nurtures in himself and in others this gift of life, given him by God. To tamper with the generative function, as I did, is to make myself a god, or to tell God, in effect, 'I know better than You do'" (p. 19). With, in her words, God "bringing me to an openness to life" (p. 20), Mrs. Kelly underwent a reverse operation to restore her procreative potential.

    And this story is by no means unique. The majority of people I know who have undergone sterilization have either had serious regrets or are now divorced!
19. C. E. Cerling, "Abortion and Contraception in Scripture," *Christian Scholars Review* 2 (1971): 58.

CHAPTER TEN: The Truth and Its Consequences

1. Stephen Clark, *Man and Woman in Christ* (Ann Arbor, MI: Servant Books, 1980), p. 98.
2. Jeremy Jackson, "Seedtime and Harvest: The Building of the Lord's House," *Life and Light* (Summer/Fall 1985): 6.
3. Harold O. J. Brown, "Not Enough Children," *Christianity Today* 29 (October 15, 1985): 10.
4. See Brown, "Not Enough Children," p. 10; and Baer and Perrotta, "Bearing Down: American Women's Declining Fertility—And Its Consequences," *Pastoral Renewal* 10 (September 1985): 25, 26.

SCRIPTURE INDEX

GENERAL INDEX

Abortion, 30, 100, 127, 130, 131
Abram (Abraham), 16, 41, 47, 48, 145
Adam, 31, 33, 34, 43, 51, 76, 77, 125, 144
Adoption, 44, 127
American Birth Control League, 18
Anarchy, 18
Anglican Church, the, 23, 140

Barrenness, 16, 47
Barth, Karl, 118
Bathsheba, 93
Bentham, Jeremy, 18
Bible, the, 25, 29, 30, 33, 45, 47, 49, 57, 65, 76, 78, 88
Birth control, birth control movement, 16, 17, 18, 19, 22, 38, 48, 93, 118
Blessings, 35, 41, 49, 61, 80, 132, 136
and commands, 40, 41

Calvin, John, 30
Canaanite woman, the, 65
Cancer, 103
Career, 19, 43, 55, 56
Celibacy, 30, 39, 85,106
Celts, the, 16
Chaunu, Pierre, 130
Childbearing, 20, 32, 39, 40, 41, 44, 48, 51, 52, 53, 57, 69, 77, 86, 87, 88, 102, 108, 113, 117, 137, 143

Childlessness, 16, 32, 44, 85, 110, 119, 120
Children, see esp. 16, 20, 21, 24, 30, 32, 34, 36, 40, 43, 44, 45, 46, 47, 48, 49, 51, 53, 60, 61, 64, 67, 70, 75, 85, 87, 88, 95, 100, 105, 107, 108, 111, 115, 116, 117, 118, 127, 132, 133, 134, 137, 144
as blessings, 16, 41, 42, 44, 45, 46, 49, 67, 70, 105, 112, 116, 119, 120, 121, 132, 134, 142, 145
of God, 62, 129
China, 16
Christ and the church, 31, 86
Church, the, 22, 23, 24, 25, 31, 38, 52, 53, 119, 128, 129, 130, 131, 132, 136
the early church, 129
Church Fathers, the, 38
Coitus interruptus, 16
Commitment, 35, 86, 89
Companionship, 33, 34
Completeness/incompleteness, 33, 48, 50
Condorcet, Marquis de, 18
Confucius, 16
Conscience, 98, 115
Consequences, 36, 53, 93, 96, 114, 121
Contraception, see esp. 10ff., 14, 15, 16, 17, 18, 19, 20, 23, 24, 25,

155